The
Adventures
of a
Mzungu

The
Adventures
of a
Mzungu

A light-hearted look at the
ups and downs of visiting Africa

DAVID ARDRON

Matador
9 Priory Business Park,
Wistow Road, Kibworth Beauchamp,
Leicestershire. LE8 0RX
Tel: 0116 279 2299
Email: books@troubador.co.uk
Web: www.troubador.co.uk/matador
Twitter: @matadorbooks

ISBN 978 1785899 560

British Library Cataloguing in Publication Data.
A catalogue record for this book is available from the British Library.

Printed and bound in the UK by TJ International, Padstow, Cornwall
Typeset in 11pt Minion Pro by Troubador Publishing Ltd, Leicester, UK

Matador is an imprint of Troubador Publishing Ltd

MIX
Paper from
responsible sources
FSC® C013056

Dedicated to the memory of Paul Brand and Selwyn Hughes, two 20th century Christian leaders whose life stories encouraged me to 'get on with it'.

CONTENTS PAGE

FOREWORD

My life has been full and varied, and if I dropped off the perch in the next few minutes I couldn't complain of the different sights I have seen, and the wide range of projects I've been involved with.

Some experiences have been a hard slog, which I thought would never end. But change comes along, sometimes expected, but quite often unexpected, like the heart attack I suffered in 2000, followed by heart surgery in 2001. Unexpected, and life-changing. For a while it seemed to be a calamity but, once recovery had taken its course, life is richer and more fulfilling than it was before. New opportunities have come along, and new experiences, many of which I never imagined could be possible.

Visits to Uganda are only one part of my life, but a major part. At the time of writing they are destined to continue for the foreseeable future. I hope that you enjoy reading about them as much as I enjoyed living them.

1.

AM I ON THE RIGHT PLANE?

Chaos and confusion reigned at Addis Ababa Airport. Chaos and confusion in a language I could not understand. The English translations of the announcements over the loudspeakers were distorted. I did not hear the flight I was waiting for mentioned at all.

I arrived at 7.30am on a flight from Heathrow, and the connection for Entebbe was scheduled for 11am. It was now well past this time and I had no idea what was happening. Planes were leaving, it seemed, for all destinations but Entebbe.

All the possible problems ran through my mind. Perhaps there had been a coup in Uganda. If there had been a coup, then planes would not be allowed to land. Perhaps there had been an accident at Entebbe and planes could not land because of the wreckage on the runway. If that was the case, then we would not be able to land until the runway had been cleared.

As I sat and waited for something to happen my mind went back to my first visit to Africa in 1990. There were twenty-seven of us and we were on the outreach element of a course. We were to spend five weeks in Africa and, as we left the plane at Nairobi Airport, I wanted to go home! Not only was that impossible, but I had no idea what God had in store for me.

I was brought back to the present by an announcement that was not clear enough to be understood, at least not by me. The other passengers waiting at gate number two stood and collected their baggage. Gate number two was the gate for the flight to Entebbe. Were we going at last? I stood, collected my belongings and followed the people.

"May we board now?" I asked a lady wearing an Ethiopian Airlines uniform. Her affirmative reply made me join the queue. I was doubtful. I had not heard the flight number announced. The man at the door checked my boarding pass and let me through. I was still doubtful. Perhaps he hadn't checked my pass properly. The lady at the head of the steps to the plane checked my boarding pass and I was on the plane. My doubts were still there. Perhaps she hadn't checked the pass properly.

I settled into my seat and fastened my seat belt. The plane taxied to the end of the runway, turned and accelerated for the take-off.

An announcement over the speaker alarmed me. "This is flight ET812," said the disembodied female voice. I sat bolt upright in shock! (Have you ever tried doing that with a seatbelt on, on a plane accelerating to take-off speed?) I was on the wrong flight! I was supposed to be on flight ET821! "Flying to Dar es Salaam," the announcement continued. By now I was in full panic. I was not going to Dar es Salaam. I was going to Entebbe. I was on the wrong flight and there was nothing I could do about it. The aircraft was by now bouncing along the runway, ready for the final thrust airwards. You cannot stop a plane in the same way as you stop a bus. There was no way I could get off. "Calling at Entebbe and Kilimanjaro," the announcement went on. What a relief! Slowly the light dawned. Two flights had been merged into one and I had not heard the announcement.

It is not easy when we are travelling alone to be sure that all the arrangements that have been made will, in fact, work out. Every Christian needs to be in touch with God at such times, and to trust Him to get us where He wishes us to go.

I settled down and began to think about the next part of my journey when I reached Entebbe. Have you noticed that, as soon as we have one worry sorted out, another worry comes into our minds? This time I was asking myself if Christine would be there to meet me.

Christine Birt and I first met when we were both students on the Crossroads Discipleship Training School course with Youth with a Mission (YWAM) at a large house called the King's Lodge just outside of Nuneaton in the early months of 1990. This course was designed for people over thirty-five years of age who had reached a 'crossroads' in their lives, and who were seeking God's will for the future.

My particular 'crossroads' was that, after nineteen years in the coal mining industry, I had been made redundant. I thought that I had better do something about the call to the mission field that I had received fifteen years previously.

Being back in a classroom after almost thirty years was quite daunting. This is not the place or the time to go into details, but we did have visiting speakers and one was Dave Duell of Colorado, USA. Dave had a healing ministry and he gave me something to think and talk about.

In 1966, as I was working in a sweet factory in Chesterfield, a lump appeared on my left foot. Lifting and carrying heavy tins of sweets around all day, every day, was hardly the best treatment for the feet. My doctor told me that I had 'flat feet', and prescribed arch supports, which I had worn until meeting Dave Duell.

Dave gave us a practical demonstration of his healing ministry, asking for volunteers. I thought I would like to volunteer and told him about my flat feet.

Dave had me sit on a chair and put my legs out. He demonstrated that my left leg was half an inch shorter than my right leg. I hadn't noticed before! As Dave was speaking I felt a movement in my thigh. When I looked at my foot it was moving! Outwards! To hear about miracles is one thing. To see one is something else. But to actually see and feel one's own leg growing is something entirely different! I immediately discarded my arch supports and have not worn them to this day.

Part of the course was to visit East Africa. We were to visit Kenya and Uganda, and we looked forward to it.

Even before she had been to Africa Christine had a sense of a call to go to Uganda. She was waiting for that call to be confirmed. At the end of our stay in Uganda twenty-six of the original twenty-seven returned home – Christine stayed on.

While we were still at Nuneaton I knew that Christine would not be returning with the group. Christine and I took a walk around the nearby country lanes one evening when she said, "When you come back from Uganda you will be leaving me behind." She told me that she was feeling God's call to that country, and I promised to keep in touch with her.

As we were crossing the border into Kenya on our way home I knew that God was speaking to me about Uganda too. I was sure that I would be returning to serve God in that country.

When Christine returned to the UK later in 1990 I paid her a visit at her flat in Knighton, Powys. I made a commitment to her ministry, to support her in prayer and finance. Christine accepted my commitment and for quite some time I took care of Christine's affairs in Britain.

Back to the aforementioned flight. We flew on towards Entebbe, which was to be the first stop. My hopes that Christine would meet me were founded on my second visit to Uganda in 1991. On that occasion there was a mix-up with flights and I was twenty-four hours late in arriving. My messages to Christine, who was meeting me, had not reached her, and she had a disappointing visit to Entebbe Airport a day too early. On that occasion I took a private hire car to Kamuli where Christine was living at the time, a distance of around 150 miles. It was expensive!

There was no mix-up this time. As I left the plane I could see Christine waving from the observation room. The immigration and customs were dealt with quickly. I had arrived for my third visit. I immediately felt at home – as though I had only been away for a few days instead of twelve months. Everything was familiar – the sights and sounds and smells. It was good to be back. To me it was confirmation that I was in the right place. The weariness of travelling faded away. There had been doubts while I waited at Addis Ababa, but now I knew that all the trials and doubts had been worthwhile. Satan would sift us as wheat and cause us to doubt and even want to turn back. That is part of his strategy to deflect us from the will of God.

A private hire car took us to Entebbe town, and we made the journey to Kamuli by public transport, changing at Kampala and Jinja. As the journey progressed I was more aware of the feeling of coming home. My host, Teddy Aketch, who had looked after me on my previous visit, welcomed me warmly. It was good to be among the Ugandan people.

2.

FIRST IMPRESSIONS

The visit to Africa as part of the Youth with a Mission (YWAM) course in 1990 was my first journey outside of the British Isles. It was also the first time I had travelled by air. We landed in Nairobi, and as we were leaving the plane, I knew that I wanted to go home. A British Airways jet (we had travelled Kenya Airways) sitting on the tarmac actually made me feel homesick!

We had five weeks in Africa in front of us. Some people pay thousands of pounds for the opportunity to visit Africa, and I wanted to go home!

We travelled by London-style black cab from the airport to the YWAM base. The countryside was flat, with dry bush. It was interesting scenery. I thought, *I'm in Africa!* But I still wanted to go home!

The base was a large house in its own grounds. It was beautiful to sit on the lawn in the warm sun, watching the little yellow finches darting around and the geckos running along the brickwork at the side of the house. We slept three to a room. It was quite like camping. Conditions were a little cramped, but as we spent most of our time outdoors or in the communal rooms of the house, it did not matter. For the first few days we spent the time rehearsing the drama scenes we were to perform on the streets.

The first visit to Kibera shantytown was quite an experience. We travelled to Kibera on a public transport bus. As the bus was crowded we were squeezed together. From my standing position I could see that many of the rivets holding the roof to the body of the bus were missing. When the bus drove over a pothole the roof and the walls parted company! I'm convinced that only the passengers were holding the bus together.

On and on we went, passing houses that would not be used as garden sheds in Britain. They were built of scraps of wood, cardboard, kerosene tins and corrugated iron; in fact, any suitable material people could find.

The bus left us in the middle of Kibera. Kibera is one of the largest shantytowns in East Africa. The sights turned into smells. Children played in the drains running along the side of the streets. Any pictures you may have seen in missionary magazines are nothing like the real thing. These shantytowns need to be experienced to understand the conditions the people are living in.

At my first open-air meeting in Africa some forty or fifty people accepted Jesus as their Saviour. A crowd gathered before we had even started. A team of Europeans in such a place was an attraction. It was a real African area. As the meeting progressed we estimated that there was a crowd of a thousand or more listening to the message.

I gave my testimony at this meeting and quickly learned that we cannot take things for granted. Part of my testimony concerns stoking a church boiler, back in Britain. I found that I had to explain what a boiler was. Central heating was beyond the understanding of our audience. In a country of perpetually high temperatures, if the weather turns cool, we simply put on more clothes! During a later visit to Kampala, when I was supposed to be more experienced, I took a bath in a hotel and, when I returned to my room, I looked around for a non-existent radiator to hang my towel over!

At the meeting we prayed for the sick. One of the men I prayed for had stomach pains. After he said the pains had gone I said, "Praise the Lord", intending to close my ministry with this man and move on. The man started speaking in tongues! After a time he stopped and I said, "Praise the Lord." He went into tongues again. This happened around six times before I realised the man thought I was telling him to praise the Lord. I did some quick thinking and said "Amen." This time he stopped!

We were encouraged by our first effort and we thanked God for the opportunity to witness as missionaries in Africa for the first time.

The YWAM base was in an area notorious for muggers and bandits. We were advised to go around in groups during the day, and not to go out after dark at all. Alarms, gates, high walls and security guards protected the neighbouring properties. The base had a security guard on patrol all night. He was a very tall Masai warrior, although he wore a guard's uniform rather than the traditional Masai dress. One evening, after dark, I needed to post a letter in the postbox outside of the office (inside the base). As I approached the postbox a deep voice boomed out of the darkness.

"Good evening," the voice said. I had almost fallen over the security guard who was sat in front of the postbox!

On a rest day most of the team went into Nairobi city to look around, leaving only a few of us at the base. I wanted to go to the local shopping centre in Hurlingham, close to where we were staying. Nobody else wanted to go and I was aware of the warnings about going out alone. I mentioned the problem to one of the ladies who worked at the base. She assured me that it would be all right to go alone as long as I did not speak to anyone and was back before dark. I felt quite adventurous as I headed towards the shopping centre. There were a number of Europeans and Americans in the shopping centre who appeared to be quite comfortable, which made me feel relaxed. I found the post office, bank, chemist and all the other shops I was likely to need. I had returned safely to the base by the time the main party had returned from Nairobi.

Part of Hurlingham was upmarket. We went door-to-door visiting one morning, inviting people to a picnic being organised by the Dove Christian Fellowship, a group based at a local school. The gates of the houses were padlocked and manned by security guards with dogs. The security men either took a leaflet from us to give to the occupiers of the houses or they fetched somebody. A good number of people attended the picnic. We gave our drama presentation, but we felt that we were entertaining the members of the local churches rather than evangelising non-Christians. Two people made commitments so the effort was worthwhile. Joy in Heaven over one sinner that repents!

On another rest day we visited the Nairobi Safari Park and pretended to be tourists. The park was home to impala, giraffe, zebra and water buffalo. The water buffalo proved to be the most exciting of the animals we saw, but we were not to know it at the time. We were travelling in a Volkswagen Microbus and driving through a remote area of the park. A water buffalo stood in the road, facing our direction. The driver, an African, stopped, and wouldn't drive any further. After a few minutes a car arrived from the opposite direction and stopped behind the water buffalo. If the beast was going to move it would be in our direction. Our driver reversed, looking for somewhere to turn the bus. We reversed until we came to a side road. We turned into the side road and travelled a different way. It was only afterwards that we learned that the water buffalo is reputed to be one of the most dangerous animals in Africa and could quite easily overturn a vehicle the size of a minibus. Little wonder that the driver was quiet. He had to get us out of the situation without alarming us!

One Sunday I preached at the Kenya City Mission Church in Nairobi. Hillary Abungu was pastor of this church. I had made contact with Hillary through a friend in Britain who had met him at a conference. We had already exchanged letters prior to my leaving Britain to travel to Africa.

The church was situated in one of Nairobi's suburbs. I preached using a microphone. As the building was quite small I could not understand why it was needed. At the end of the service I stood outside the church building, shaking hands with the congregation as they left. I could hear music playing from a loudspeaker on the outside wall of the building. It was then that I realised what the microphone was for. The neighbourhood had heard my sermon whether they had wanted to or not!

3.

DID YOU HEAR A LION ROAR?

It was a pleasant but tiring journey from Nairobi to Eldoret by coach. The coach was more comfortable than the bus from Nairobi to the site of our first open-air meeting, but could not be termed 'luxury'. The journey took around seven hours. We saw cranes and zebra at the side of the road.

We established ourselves in the New Miyako Hotel at Eldoret. It was very, very noisy on the streets outside. Traffic was constant from 5am 'til midnight and, as in all African towns, the most important component of the motor vehicle was the horn!

We worked with a church in a new village named Roadblock, which was being built to accommodate workers at an industrial estate just outside of Eldoret. The houses were modern by African standards, not unlike the British prefab type of house of the post-war era, with large plots of land between each house for the residents to grow food. Chickens ran around and goats were tethered on the grass areas.

We visited door-to-door in Roadblock. We spoke to the people, inviting them to a crusade we were to hold at the end of the week at the local shopping centre. The villagers did not see Europeans very often and some of the children were frightened of us. We visited the village most days that week and had several conversations. A number of people accepted Jesus, but a lot of the villagers seemed to be Christians but had not received the Holy Spirit. We prayed for them to receive the Spirit. When Paul visited Ephesus, as recorded in Acts chapter 19, verses 1 to 8, he discovered Christians who had not yet received the Holy Spirit, and he prayed for them to receive. In the same way, we prayed for the people of Roadblock who believed but had not yet received God's Spirit. We also prayed for the sick. I prayed for a man who had malaria. His condition reminded me to keep on taking my own anti-malarial tablets.

The time came for our crusade in the shopping centre. This was not a shopping centre in the European sense. There was only one shop! No post office, no supermarket, and no chemist. Only one shop which sold almost everything. It was the place where people gathered and the place we should be to tell the good news about Jesus. We set up the equipment on a large open space in front of the shop. We presented our programme, and on this occasion it was my privilege to present the message. The local pastor called for those who wished to receive Jesus for the first time to come forward. Almost the entire congregation moved towards us seeking salvation! All that could be seen was a sea of faces. One of our team members, whilst still in Nuneaton, had seen a vision of a crescent moon over an African village, and there it was, in the sky, a crescent moon!

On our rest day Christine Birt and I paid a visit to a school around twelve miles outside of Eldoret. The school was run by the Africa Inland Mission. Nic Birt, Christine's son, had worked at the school for ten months in 1988. The school was around six miles from the village of Iten. The children were on holiday on the day we visited, but we did meet the headmistress, a Canadian lady named Heather, and Pauline, a teacher from Folkestone. The school building was set in beautiful countryside, surrounded by mountains, with a waterfall behind the property. It was bush country, with snakes in the grass and monkeys in the trees. Eagles circled looking for their dinners. They swooped down to catch rabbits, rats or snakes. Eagles were also to be seen circling where a lion had killed an animal, waiting for the lion to eat its fill and leave the body. It is a magnificent sight to see these majestic birds soaring in the sky, bringing to mind Isaiah chapter 40, verse 31. It is good to be reminded that, if we put our hope in the Lord, our strength will be renewed, and we will soar on wings like eagles, without growing weary, and walk without fainting. We need to be constantly reminded that we walk in God's strength, especially when we are working in intense heat and need to travel long distances.

We travelled to the school by public transport, which dropped us outside the school premises. The vehicle was a normal estate car, the size of a Ford Cortina. It carried thirteen of us! Four people sat in the front seats (two in the driver's seat!) and four people (including Christine and I) in the seats behind. Three people sat in an extra row of seats behind the normal back seats, and two more people in the crumple zone (the area between the rear seats and the rear window). The vehicle travelled at high speed, on a winding road down the side of the Rift Valley!

On our return to Eldoret Christine and I walked for six miles uphill, but we were rewarded by beautiful views over the Rift Valley. At one point Christine said, "Did you hear a lion roar then?"

"No," I answered. "I didn't hear anything."

A little while later we both heard what definitely sounded like a lion's roar! So we walked along, keeping our eyes open for this 'lion'. There was a sudden flash of lightning in the distance followed by a rumble of thunder, which sounded just like the roar of a lion! Christine asked me if I knew what to do if I met a lion.

When I said that I didn't, she told me, "You thump it on the nose and then run away whilst it's still startled." I could just see myself thumping a lion on the nose and then running away!

It is well to learn to be flexible when working in Africa. One morning we went into Roadblock to hold teaching seminars for new converts. First we had to walk around the village inviting people to attend the meeting. There were more children than adults, and most of the adults were not yet Christians. The meeting was quickly changed to an evangelistic talk. I think that one person came forward to accept salvation and a number came for healing. I prayed for one man who said he had a stomach ulcer. He claimed later that the pain had gone away.

4.

SO, THIS IS UGANDA

The road from Eldoret to Malaba was very bumpy and the full-sized bus we travelled on was driven very carefully. Some of the potholes were almost large enough to swallow the bus, and we had to leave the road at some points to drive along the verge.

At Malaba we crossed the border into Uganda. It was very, very hot! Getting through the border took a long time. I had my luggage searched, but the customs man got fed up partway through.

He kept on saying, "It's too hot! It's too hot!" Then he threw his arms up in the air and said, "Oh, go on." I thought that if the weather was too hot for the local people then I wouldn't stand a chance.

The road on the Ugandan side of the border was better. Uganda is a beautiful country, with lush vegetation. There are lots of colourful birds flying around and we saw a family of baboons. A crane came close by me one day, and it is not uncommon to see vultures perched in the trees and on the edges of buildings.

The people were responsive. We went door-to-door visiting in Jinja and people were saved. Quite a number promised to attend church the following Sunday. I must point out that in all this evangelistic work we had local church leaders with us who took names and addresses. We didn't 'hit and run'!

On our first Sunday we visited a local Pentecostal church for morning service. The pastor asked all the visitors to stand and say where we had come from. The sermons, both in Kenya and Uganda, were preached in two or more languages. Sometimes I listened to the wrong interpreter and found that I did not understand what was being said! At one church there appeared to be several little groups of people holding conversations whilst I was preaching, and I asked my interpreter if they were holding their own meetings. I was told that they were all from different tribes and that somebody was interpreting my sermon into their own languages.

We were placed on work duties whilst at the YWAM base at Jinja, and part of my duties was to paint the walls and gates. I also drove the base minibus and pickup truck, which I enjoyed more than the painting!

The pickup had no handbrake or rear-view mirror. When I wanted to know if there was anything following me I had to put my head out of the window and take a look! The truck was used to bring cane from a sugar plantation to make shelters in the base grounds. These shelters were to be used for students to study under, or to just relax under in free periods. I was to enjoy a cup of tea under one of the shelters when I paid a return visit to the base in 1992.

Driving the minibus was not without incidents. There was a team of German students staying at the YWAM town base in Jinja. On my first drive into the town I took these students back to their base, as they had been visiting our base, and we ran out of petrol! There we were, fourteen of us pushing a minibus (a Toyota Hiace) to the nearest petrol station. It was around a mile to the filling station, but it felt double the distance in the heat.

On another trip I took a team to Jinja Prison. There were armed guards outside. Whilst the team was in the prison I did a few more runs, including a little door-to-door ministry. By the time I returned to the prison to collect the team it was dark. It felt strange to be driving through the gates and along a dark track to the centre of the prison. The track was around three quarters of a mile long, and there didn't appear to be a soul around. There was an eerie atmosphere, as though time had stood still. I felt as though I was driving through a dream. I had the feeling that eyes were watching me, and that I would either be hijacked by escaped prisoners or stopped and searched by guards.

As we returned to the base we stopped in the town centre to allow members of the group to visit the shops. I parked the bus beneath a lamppost. It was eight o'clock in the evening and it was dark. As a few of us were waiting inside the bus sparks started to fly around the vehicle. When I looked up I could see that the lamppost was swaying and touching the overhead electric cables! We decided to leave the van. As I clambered out I caught my foot in the seat belt and found myself sprawling on the road!

Somebody shouted, "It's a coup; it's a coup!" The sound of the crackling of the cables against the lamppost sounded similar to gunfire! One of the men in the team heard the shouting, saw me sprawled out on the road, and thought I'd been shot!

One day, as I was alone in the bus leaving Jinja, an armed policeman stepped into the road and stopped me. When I first drove the base vehicles I asked if there were any strange local laws that I should know about, and was told, "No, just give way to anything bigger"! I wondered if I had broken some law that I didn't know about, and I wished that I had an African with me.

The policeman looked at me, grinned, and asked, "Will you give me a lift?"

I looked at his gun and thought to myself, I'd better not say, "No".

I gave him a lift for around half a mile to the next roadblock. Needless to say, I didn't have any trouble getting through the roadblock!

During one weekend I decided to fast for personal reasons. I had my breakfast on Saturday morning and my next meal was at teatime on Sunday. During tea the dining room leader gave the announcements. Monday, the day following, was to be a fast day for the base! Oh no! As it happened, I spent Monday away from the base. Members of our team were to spend a week at a village named Nawanjago, eighteen miles from Jinja. I was nominated the driver to take them, and those travelling were exempt from fasting!

There was a church at Nawanjago founded by George Mwigo, a politician in President Milton Obote's second government. George became a Christian whilst in prison after President Yoweri Museveni had overthrown Obote. Christine Birt was one of the team members who went to Nawanjago. It was here, during the week, that she received confirmation of her calling to Uganda. Before visiting this village she had almost decided to return to Britain with us as she was finding the weather too hot. During a prayer meeting, Christine looked up, and her eyes met the eyes of one of the Nawanjago church leaders, and she knew that she would be staying. The desire to stay had overwhelmed the difficulty with the hot weather.

A large earth grader arrived at the base one day to level out the road leading to the main road. The machine set down a blade, not unlike a snowplough, and skimmed off the top layer of the red earth road in order to make the road smooth. In the early hours of the following morning I heard the sound of car wheels spinning. It was similar to the sound made when a vehicle is stuck in the snow in Britain. We did not have snow, but we had had rain during the night and the road had turned into a swamp. The base leader was attempting to reach the main road with a four-wheel drive truck, and was failing. As it was a Sunday a number of us had preaching appointments in various churches in Jinja. Later in the morning the hot sun dried the road enough to allow the truck to travel. We kept our appointments.

On another occasion I preached at the Church of the Redeemed in Jinja. After the meeting I walked to the bus park to catch my bus back to Wairaka, the suburb of Jinja where the YWAM base was located. As I walked across the park I heard a voice calling, "David!" Being in a strange town on a strange continent I ignored the voice, thinking that it could not possibly be me that the man wanted. As the calling became insistent I thought I had better investigate, and I turned around. A bus conductor was calling me by name, and it was definitely me that he wanted! Upon reaching the bus I discovered that Helen, one of our team members who had been preaching at another church, was on board. Helen had spotted me walking across the park, realised that I had walked by the bus that I needed, and had asked the conductor to call me.

5.

GOOD OLD LAND ROVER!

Whilst visiting towns in Uganda, if a person is staying overnight, or for a period of time, it is necessary to report to certain officials to let them know that a visitor is in the town, and to let the officials know the purpose of the visit. In Kamuli, forty miles north of Jinja, where Christine Birt settled for the early years of her ministry in Uganda, the Security Officer registers any visitors. It is also advisable to pay a courtesy call on the District Administrator.

The first time I visited Kamuli, the District Administrator was a saved man. He was named Hillary, and Christine and I visited Hillary and his wife, Rose, in their home where we enjoyed a beautiful time of fellowship. We held a prayer time together and Hillary laughed in the Spirit. It was infectious, and we all laughed for a long time. As Christine and I left the house, and walked along the driveway, we could see Hillary silhouetted in a window – still laughing!

A large part of Christine's ministry was to Kamuli Prison. My first visit to this prison came in 1991. The Miracle Centre (the church Christine worked with) had recently begun this outreach work, and my first visit was their third visit. The pastor of the church, Pastor Gabriel, was with us and I had assumed that he would be preaching.

Imagine my surprise when, as we walked through the gate into the prison, the pastor put his hand on my shoulder and said, "You are preaching!" I don't remember anything about the sermon, but I do remember that it was a blessing both to the prisoners and to myself.

Christine also made regular visits to Bugungu Prison, near Jinja. Quite a lot of the prisoners at Bugungu were dressed in rags and had some difficulty in covering their bodies and hiding their embarrassment. There is a real need for tee shirts and shorts in all of the prisons in Uganda, and also for medicines. Christine seeks to minister to the body as well as to the soul, but the surface can only be scratched with her limited resources.

Bugungu is on a peninsula which juts out into Lake Victoria, and the best way to reach the village is by means of a longboat across the lake from Jinja port. A longboat is made of planks of wood with dovetail joints at the ends. The floor is also made of planks of wood. The basic design has not changed for many years. The commercial longboats, which travel across Lake Victoria, carry eight or nine passengers and are paddled by two men. On one journey Christine picked up a spare paddle that was lying on the floor of the boat and paddled along with the men. I think that she was more of a hindrance than help, but the ferrymen were too polite to say so! Around midway across the lake I whispered to Christine that I couldn't swim.

She was quiet for a moment or two, and then said, "Now you tell me!"

My first experience in a longboat was on Lake Kyoga in 1991. Christine had helped in baptising thirty new converts in the lake, and I had been taking photographs from the longboat. After the baptismal service we were taken for a ride on the lake. The boat leaked, and our feet were covered in water. A fish flapped around in the bottom of the boat!

One popular method of travel around Uganda is by taxi. The taxis are minibuses, which run on set routes but without any timetable. They start their journeys once they are full. The most popular vehicle for a taxi is the Toyota Hiace. They are licensed to carry fourteen passengers, but with a driver and conductor, the number of people they can legally carry is sixteen. Sometimes, especially in bush areas, the vehicles are pickup trucks or saloon cars.

During one journey, in 1991, Christine and I climbed into the back of a pickup in Kamuli Taxi Park. We were asked to leave it and climbed into a minibus, but the gatekeeper refused to let the minibus leave the park. We passengers got out, left the park and walked to the marketplace, and boarded a Land Rover. As we travelled along I sat in the back of the Land Rover thinking that this was the best vehicle I had travelled in whilst in Africa. Good old Land Rover! Christine, being a European lady, had the privilege of riding up front with the driver, and she could see what I could not see. On the floor, between her feet, was a plastic container of petrol sloshing around, with a tube leading into the engine! We reached our destination, and the driver pulled a cigarette out of his pocket and placed it in his mouth. Christine was up and out of the Land Rover before it had fully stopped!

Normally, in Uganda, domestic animals, such as dogs and cats, are left to fend for themselves. They are not regarded as pets and are expected to do useful things like catch mice and rats and generally scavenge for their food. Animals owned by Europeans fare better. Christine buys fish for her cats and meat for her dogs.

There is a law in Uganda, which states that all domestic dogs must be vaccinated against rabies and a certificate must be shown on demand. Christine, on one occasion, was attacked and bitten by a pack of dogs and it was eight days before she could obtain an anti-rabies vaccine for herself. There are a lot of stray dogs loose in Uganda and rabies is a major problem.

Jinja is Uganda's second largest town and sits on the north shore of Lake Victoria, which is either the second or third largest lake in the world depending on which geography book you read. One day we went to Jinja to have Christine's cat, Sanyu, spayed. Sanyu had already given birth to three kittens and Christine thought that it was enough. In Britain, when a cat is taken for spaying, it is left with the vet, still alert, and collected again after the operation is over and the cat has recovered. It isn't so in Uganda. Christine and I had to comfort Sanyu whilst the injections were given. I wondered if I would have to watch the whole operation!

After the cat was sedated the vet said, "You can go now; come back in two hours." I was the first out of the door! I am squeamish, as any nurse taking a sample of my blood for testing would tell you, and I very badly needed fresh air at that point!

As with most rural communities, when a visit is made to the local large town or city, there are many visits and calls to be made. So we took advantage whilst Sanyu was being spayed. One of the things we had to do was to apply for Christine's Ugandan driving licence.

The counter clerk at the Revenue Office looked at Christine's British licence and asked, "What language is this?" Christine's previous home in Britain, before moving to Uganda, was in Wales, and there was a Welsh translation on her driving licence. As anybody who has driven in Wales and seen the road signs will know, our eyes automatically go to the Welsh bits! The lady at the Revenue Office had not even heard of Wales!

A few years later, a Welsh friend of mine was preaching in a church in Uganda when she realised that the interpreter was translating into English. She asked him what language he was translating into.

"English," he replied.

"But I thought that I was speaking English," she said.

"Yes," he replied. "But you are speaking funny English!"

The time came to collect Sanyu, and Christine and I took her back to Kamuli by taxi. Sanyu was a little unsteady for a few days, but she was soon normal again.

During one visit to Jinja we visited the AIDS ward of a hospital where YWAM had a ministry to the patients. It was sad to see people who knew that they were dying and yet had no faith in God to face eternity. A number accepted Jesus and made their peace with God, but most were very frightened. I am now, as I write this later, in a position to have personally known people who have died of AIDS in Uganda. Like Joy, who was Christine's house girl when I visited Kamuli in August 1992. Joy was fit on this occasion and did not seem to have anything wrong with her. When

I made a further visit to Kamuli in November of the same year, Joy was seriously ill. By Christmas she was dead.

After visiting the AIDS ward Christine and I visited the YWAM town base for lunch and to attend a fellowship meeting for AIDS outpatients. During the meeting the leader led a long prayer in Luganda, the Ugandan national language. (Although English is the business language, there are also almost a hundred tribal languages, as well as Swahili, which is spoken in areas close to the border with Kenya.) A long prayer in a language you can follow can be boring, but when you do not know what is being said, it can be deadly! When I woke up I found that my glasses had fallen onto the floor! I don't think that anybody had noticed!

Kasambira is a village on the Kamuli to Jinja road. When I first visited the Miracle Centre in this village the church was just one week old. Sam, a young man whom I had met at Kamuli the previous year, was pastor. This was Sam's first charge. I prepared to preach on 'Jesus Christ – greater than Moses'. When I arrived at the village I was told that a cult, which emphasised the Law of Moses, had been working in the area!

Upon return to Kamuli I discovered that Christine had a sore foot. Earlier in the day she had fallen into one of the deep drains that ran at the side of the road. At the time of the fall there did not appear to be any injury, but after I had left for Kasambira Christine's foot had become painful. It was apparent that the foot was sprained, but after prayer and a night's rest it had healed enough to enable her to accompany me to Kasambira the following day.

One afternoon I ministered at the Busoga Girls' School in Kamuli. Forty girls attended the Christian Union meeting and, when I made a call for prayer, thirty-eight of them came forward! I encouraged them to pray for each other in pairs.

The people of Uganda are hungry for the word of God, and are always willing to listen. As Christine and I walked through Kamuli one day a group of fourteen men stopped us and asked how to be saved. Christine preached a mini sermon and all accepted Jesus. Quite often, as Christine holds conversations with people, they are saved in the street.

On one occasion, after seeing me off at Entebbe Airport on my return to the UK, Christine took a private hire car to Kampala and the driver received Christ as they travelled along.

We sometimes travelled by bus rather than taxi. Buses are full-sized single-deckers, which run on set routes and have timetables. They are generally cheaper but slower than taxis. The timetables are more fiction than fact! One day I waited for a bus in the village of Namwendra, where I had been ministering, to travel to Bulopa, to meet up with Christine who had been ministering in that village. I waited, and waited, then the bus arrived ninety minutes late!

Christine and I ministered together at Bulopa the following day. We waited at the bus stop for the bus to Kamuli, where we were based, and sat at the side of the road. After three hours had passed we started to make plans to spend another night in Bulopa when the bus raced into the village followed by a dust storm. Chickens flew in all directions!

Christine took me to visit Isisi, a mud hut village on the shores of Lake Kyoga. This time the bus was four hours late! The trip was memorable as we travelled deep into the jungle for fifty miles in first and second gear. The night fell as we were still travelling, and we saw a wolf illuminated in the headlamps of the bus.

A hawker was selling charcoal at one of the many stops. A passenger on the bus, who claimed to have been short-measured on a previous journey, grabbed the hawker and began to beat him, hitting the hawker's head against one of the supporting poles of the bus!

Christine pushed herself between them and shouted, "Stop! Stop! In the Name of Jesus, stop!" I don't know whether it was the Name of Jesus that did it, or the torch that Christine was shining into the man's eyes, but he immediately stopped beating the hawker!

As we drew near to the end of our journey we entered a heavily mosquito-infested area, and Christine dressed up. She was already wearing a gomice (a long African dress which reached the ankles) and a pullover to cover her arms. She now put a shawl over her head, which was held in position with an imitation miner's lamp fastened to her forehead by an elastic strap. She looked like a sheik! She looked so funny that I burst out laughing, and that made her laugh too! When we looked along the bus the African passengers were watching us, all with straight faces, and that made us laugh all the more!

We reached the village of Isisi at eleven o'clock. It was very dark. The word had gone around the village that two mzungus (white people) had arrived on the bus, and dozens of children had come out to greet us. We walked along a path from Isisi to another village around half a mile away. The night seemed to grow darker and darker. We arrived at the second village and came across a large building. It proved to be a mud-walled church building with a thatched roof. It was dark outside, and not much lighter inside. Oil lamps gave just enough light to see, once our eyes grew accustomed. It was full of people; all we could see was white teeth. It was a relief to go to bed and wait for daylight.

6.

OOPS!

During one of my six-week stays in Uganda, a team from the Monmouth-based Living Water Ministries paid a visit. The team conducted evangelistic rallies and teaching seminars in Kamuli and Kampala. They consisted of Paul and Tricia Humberstone, and Becci Lovell. Becci had a singing ministry and had released work on the Chapel Lane record label. Paul was the pastor of a church in Monmouth.

During a previous visit to Britain, Christine Birt had spent some time in Monmouth, at the home of a member of Paul's church. I needed to visit Christine to discuss some matters, so I telephoned her.

"Where will you be at twelve o'clock on Sunday?" I asked her.

"In the King's Head," Christine replied.

"You what?" I queried.

"In the King's Head," she repeated, and then went on, "It's a pub."

It sounded so funny coming from teetotal Christine. She explained that Paul's church did not have their own building, and met in a room above the pub!

Christine and I met the team at Entebbe Airport and we spent the night at the Namirembe Guest House in Kampala. The following morning we wished to visit Robert

Karanja, who was the leader of the Miracle Centre Church in Uganda and had his headquarters in Kampala. We didn't know how to get there, and as we were discussing it, a knock came on the door of the room we were in. It was a British man who we knew slightly, named David. Robert Karanja wanted to meet us and had sent David to invite us! God knows our needs, and sometimes our prayers are answered before we even ask!

After our visit to Robert Karanja, David drove us to Jinja where he had business at the YWAM base. God does indeed answer prayer and brings the right people into our lives at just the right time.

On the first day the team was in Kamuli, I accompanied them to the village of Kyamuluya where Paul spoke to the church leaders and prayed for their faith to be anointed. One of the men I prayed with went into a trancelike state and I became really concerned for him. The man did not respond to anything I was saying to him. I discovered later that the only issue was that he couldn't understand English, and that he wasn't really in a trance!

The team visited an orphanage run by the Church of Uganda (Anglican) at Lugazi, on the road from Jinja to Kampala. This orphanage took children between the age of five and twelve. The children had mostly been abandoned by their mothers as babies and spent four years being fostered before coming to Lugazi. At the age of twelve they went on to another place for further education. The children were exposed to the Gospel, and the high standard of education allowed many of the students to go on to university and to a better standard of life than they would have had if their mothers had struggled to try to keep them.

Whilst in Kamuli the team distributed light medicines and children's clothing to some of the poorer families, but the stronger medicines were handed to a doctor who was working with the German version of Voluntary Service Overseas. The doctor was very grateful.

Teaching seminars for church leaders were held in the mornings in a hired room at Kamuli Teacher Training College. Around three dozen church leaders from villages surrounding the town attended. The leaders were to take the teaching back to their own churches. Times of ministry for healing and anointing were held, with a number of pastors, secretaries and other leaders being delivered from past hurts, bad habits and sin that hadn't been repented of. Church leaders need to be right with God before they can help those entrusted to their charge.

Gospel crusades were held in the evenings on the town's football field. I took part in sketches and gave testimonies. In one sketch I was the beggar at Gate Beautiful, and in another, the Good Samaritan. It was all good fun. The Africans love to see acting.

Then we moved on to Kampala. My first visit to Uganda's capital was in 1990 with the YWAM Crossroads team. We had hired a bus for a day trip to visit Entebbe Zoo and the Missionary Aviation Fellowship office in Kampala. On the journey to Kampala the bus broke down, with clouds of steam erupting from the radiator. When a replacement bus arrived the bus company tried to charge extra for using two vehicles!

Patrick Musoke arranged the ministry in Kampala for the team from Monmouth. Patrick was the pastor of the Agape Christian Outreach Centre, and the fellowship met in a room at the Tween Age School in the Makerere district of Kampala, close to Makerere University. The headmistress of the school was a member of Patrick's church.

The team did much the same things in Kampala as they had done in Kamuli. The teaching seminars for church leaders were held in the Public Library hall on Bombo Road, which had been hired for the week. Ministry was given to help people to put themselves right with God. I prayed for a lady and went to put my fingers on her forehead. My fingers were still two inches away from the lady's forehead when a charge of electricity shot through my body, along my arm and into my fingertips. The lady's feet left the ground and she shot backwards, and onto the ground with a thump! All I could say was, "Oops!"

The Living Water Ministries team was staying in a different part of Kampala from where I was staying. I was spending the week in a guesthouse at Bugalubi, and I had to find my way into the city centre and out again, daily, to the Public Library and to the place where the Gospel crusades were being held. It was good training for me and I later felt that I could find my way around Kampala. There is nothing like being alone in a strange city for getting to know it.

Kampala's taxi park is a frightening-looking place at first. There are more than 300 minibuses crowded together. Some display destinations boards, but most do not, so it is a question of asking the conductors where they are going. The taxi I needed always seemed to be parked at the opposite side of the park, no matter where I started from or where I wanted to go!

The evening Gospel meetings were held in the Makerere district, and one day I decided to walk there, as I wanted to see more of the city. Somebody in the city centre pointed vaguely in the direction I should follow and I set off along Bombo Road. I walked and walked, and when I found myself outside the gates of Makerere University I knew I had walked too far. At least I knew where I was, and it was only a question of walking along Makerere Road to find the road that led to the site for the meeting.

The Gospel meetings at Makerere were much the same as they had been in Kamuli. One evening we prayed for a woman who had been dumb since she had given birth to twins three years previously. The problem was not with her voice as she could make noises, but with her jaw. Her jaw was stiff for some reason. Upon our advice the lady began to exercise her jaw. This happened for two or three evenings, and then she spoke! The first word she said was, "Yesu" (Jesus).

Kampala, late at night, is not very pleasant. It is wise to be indoors before darkness falls. Europeans and Americans are targets for muggers and thieves. One evening, the meeting at Makerere finished later than intended. A local church leader escorted Christine, who had joined us later in the week and was staying in the same guesthouse as I was, and me to the taxi park, and was trying to make us hurry as he was very much aware of the danger we were in. Christine insisted on stopping to look in shop windows and the poor man was very frustrated. He was visibly relieved after he had seen us onto the taxi for Bugalubi.

There was danger even in the daytime. Both Christine and I have had bags slashed in Kampala on separate occasions. On one visit, when I was staying with Patrick, I was alone in Patrick's flat whilst he was out shopping. I heard gunfire outside. I wondered what I was supposed to do if Patrick was the one who had been shot! Don't forget to pray for the safety of any missionaries you know personally.

At one time, back in Britain, an African was staying at the home of a friend in Mansfield, and I asked him if he was sleeping well. He replied that he was, but that he had heard gunfire the previous evening. I thought that it was strange as we have very little problems with gunfire in Mansfield, but said nothing. It was only later that I remembered that it was November, the time of the year when the British celebrate a failed attempt to blow up the Houses of Parliament, and that it must have been fireworks that he had heard!

7.

MY FIRST SNAKE

My fourth visit to Uganda came as an unexpected bonus. It enabled me to visit Uganda on two occasions within six months. I had already made a visit flying with Ethiopian Airlines using the wait-listed return flight arrangement. Upon trying to arrange my return flight to Britain I discovered that the flight I wanted was fully booked, which wasn't too much of a problem as it is one of the risks of using the wait list. It is just a question of being booked onto the next available flight. Then I discovered the problem. All the flights were fully booked for several weeks!

As I could not be in Uganda for that long a time I booked a flight to Britain using British Airways. This meant that I had two unused return tickets; one for each direction! Of course I could not waste them, so I made my fourth visit.

I never saw Christine Birt on this occasion as she had gone to Kabale in southwest Uganda to take care of a church. The wife of the pastor of the church in Kabale had died, and Christine was giving the pastor the opportunity of taking time off. It did not affect my visit as I had a good relationship with the church leaders in Kamuli, who welcomed me and arranged my ministry. Pastor Gabriel was the leader of the church, assisted by Okumu

Wilberforce, and Teddy Aketch was my host. Teddy was a local government official as well as being a church leader.

On my first evening, for this visit, I was at the home of Okumu Wilberforce, when all of a sudden there was a loud bang, and the lights went out! A power substation nearby had exploded. Welcome back! The area was without power for a number of days before the electricity company was able to complete repairs.

I paid a couple of visits to Kamuli Prison during this three-week trip. Some of the prisoners I had seen a few months previously, but there were a number of new faces. Prison is a mobile community, so evangelism is an ongoing outreach. I met with the officer in charge of the prison and he shared with me some of the needs of the prisoners. These included shorts and tee-shirts, blankets, soap, toothpaste and medicines. The prisoners also needed lotions for skin diseases, plasters and bandages. Bibles, writing materials and educational books were also on the list. Government funds cover a basic meal each day, usually rice, but very little else. The prisoners rely on their families for their other needs. Too often the families are poor and live too far away from the prison. They do not have spare money for the extra items needed in prison. Christians in other lands take the place of the families and help to provide the extra items, but only the surface is being scratched.

Some of the prisoners were being held simply on an accusation. On one occasion, whilst I was in Uganda, a prisoner who had been on remand for eight years appeared in court only to have the case thrown out by the magistrate. Eight years for nothing! And no compensation!

I spent two days preaching at Kasambira, a village on the Kamuli to Jinja road. There was a caretaker pastor at the time, as Sam, the pastor of the church, was in hospital in Bulopa suffering from sleeping sickness. Sleeping sickness is a disease transmitted by the tsetse fly, and can be fatal in its advanced stages.

I visited Sam in hospital in Bulopa. He had almost recovered from sleeping sickness and was expecting to be discharged from hospital within the following week. I was preaching in the village later in the day, and Sam was well enough to attend the meeting, along with his mother. I got into Sam's mother's good books by asking if she was his sister!

The journey back to Kamuli after this particular meeting was quite something. I began the journey by riding on the back of a bicycle owned by a member of the Bulopa church. Most of the bicycles in Uganda have a seat over the rear wheel to enable a passenger to ride pillion. The roads are crowded with bicycles carrying two people. A cycle and driver can be hired, and this form of transport is called boda-boda. Boda men plying for hire can normally be found at taxi parks, bus stations and at other places where people congregate. It is a cheap and handy form of transport to travel across a town.

I set off on my journey from Bulopa to Kamuli riding on the back of a bicycle. Part of the way along the road to Namwendra, which was a village we had to pass through, a bus came along behind us. I got off the bicycle and onto the bus. I got off the bus at Namwendra and waited for a bus to Kamuli. Whilst I was waiting, a pickup truck pulled up alongside me. A European man was driving. The man offered me a lift to Kamuli and I climbed into the back of the pickup. I did not know who he was, and as I was in the back of the truck, we could not talk. Nobody in Kamuli to whom I described the man seemed to know who he was. Uganda is a country with a lot of need, and it is possible for various missions to be working in an area without meeting each other. The projects seem to complement each other rather than compete, which is one of God's miracles. God knows where everybody is, and what they are doing.

It was always a privilege to preach at the Miracle Centre in Kamuli. I preached at this church on one occasion and was told afterwards that I had preached for ninety minutes without faltering! It is good when the Holy Spirit takes over. I certainly did not have enough preaching notes for ninety minutes!

Although I was almost halfway through the visit, the Kamuli Miracle Centre held a welcome party for me. It was an enjoyable time, with lots of food and speeches. One of the elders of the church, Kafco, who was a local businessman, offered the use of a vehicle for some of the journeys I had to make. This was an answer to prayer. Due to the rate of exchange being lower than expected I thought that it might be necessary to curtail some of my journeys. That would have meant a cancellation of some of my ministry.

The rate of exchange was going down almost daily. When I called at the bank at Entebbe Airport upon arrival for this particular visit I was shocked at the way the rate had fallen since my previous visit a few months earlier.

A week later, when I changed money in Jinja, the rate had fallen even further. The pound was taking a heavy battering in many parts of the world at that time. I had to be careful with the money I had. The costs of this visit had been estimated on the basis of my previous visit. I was only in Uganda for three weeks. It would have been difficult for full-time missionaries, who were depending upon funds from the United Kingdom, to see the value of the gifts from their supporters reduce in size in a matter of weeks. We need to be aware of this in our giving to missions. The exchange rates are not always static. Of course, things can go the other way too. The exchange rate can be beneficial to the missionary. World money markets do not just affect businesses and holidaymakers, as the media reports. Missionaries and aid agencies are affected too.

On one occasion I preached at Namwendra, on Exodus chapter 6, verses 2 to 13, wherein God promises deliverance. This turned out to be apt as I was stranded in the village due to the meeting finishing late. Taxis served Namwendra from Kamuli, but by the time the meeting had finished, the last taxi to Kamuli for the day had gone. I realised that I would have to spend the night in the village. I was not happy about the situation. As I had no intention of spending a night away from my base at Kamuli I had no change of clothes or toilet kit with me. I'm the sort of person who is naturally scruffy, but I knew that I would look even scruffier the following day. I don't like that! I know that God looks on the inside rather than the outside but I do like to make an effort, even in the middle of Africa!

God does deliver! I was eating supper at around 10pm,

and feeling far from happy, when Kafco appeared with his pickup truck! Teddy, my host in Kamuli, knew that I had intended to return to Kamuli and had called Kafco, who had come to find me.

Pastor Gabriel and I made two visits to Kasolwe, which was a trading centre for nomadic cattle herders. We made the first visit in Kafco's truck, for a Sunday service. A church had been planted at the trading centre to serve the cattle herders, who did not have a settled home. Some people had settled at Kasolwe and had established a village. Six people went forward for salvation at the end of the meeting.

On the following Wednesday, Pastor Gabriel and I made a return visit to Kasolwe. We sat in a pickup truck in Kamuli Taxi Park for nearly three hours before we started our journey. The pastor was just about to abandon the trip as time was passing, when the driver started the journey.

As we journeyed the rain began to pour. This rain was out of season, and was seen as a gift from God. There was a shortage of water in Kamuli at this time. The tap in Teddy's yard was dry, and water had to be brought from a borehole. Teddy's two daughters, Yvonne and Yvette, fetched water very early in the morning, before going to school. Rainwater in this area is pure. There is no industry to pollute it. When the rain comes buckets and bowls are put out to catch the precious liquid.

The attendance at the meeting at Kasolwe, being a Wednesday, was a lot less than on the Sunday. Most of the men were out with the cattle, leaving only the women and children to attend the Bible study. Pastor Gabriel and I had an enjoyable time, both in the Bible study and in the time of fellowship that followed. Public transport for our return to Kamuli seemed to be virtually non-existent, but a truck owned by Action Aid gave us a lift.

I made a visit to Nawanjago on the Kamuli to Jinja road. As I waited for a taxi to return to Kamuli, a pickup truck stopped and the driver offered me a lift. The driver wanted to know what I was doing in Uganda, so I told him. He informed me that he was a priest of the Noah's sect. I discovered later that this cult preached that white people could not be saved. I wondered what the priest thought about me!

Nawanjago was the village Christine had visited with the YWAM team in 1990, when her call to remain in Uganda was confirmed. She took me to visit Nawanjago in 1991, and when the time came to return to Kamuli, we got lifts on two motorcycles. As we stood at the side of the road, waiting for a taxi, the two motorcycles came along. One of the motorcycles went by without stopping, but the second screeched to a halt. Christine and I were surprised to find that the rider was British. The first rider, also British, realised that his colleague was no longer following him and returned. The two riders gave us lifts to Kamuli and came into Teddy's house to join us for coffee. They told us they were working with Voluntary Service Overseas on a two-year project with local schools.

One taxi ride out to Nawanjago was another experience. The taxi left Kamuli Taxi Park with only a few passengers on board and I thought that we were leaving early. Normally, taxis do not leave the taxi park until they are full. Then came the experience. We spent the next forty-five minutes driving around Kamuli, competing with another taxi, touting for passengers. On the return journey, at one point I counted twenty-five passengers in the fourteen-seater taxi.

There was a real hunger for the word of God in Nawanjago, as there is in all the other villages. The people want more than can be given in short visits. I could have stayed much longer in every village visited and still not have satisfied the hunger. It broke my heart to have to leave.

Patrick Musoke, our contact in Kampala, paid a surprise visit one evening. Patrick had received a letter from Paul Humberstone, who was the leader of Living Water Ministries in Monmouth. Paul had asked Patrick to contact me in Kamuli and ask me to look at some land in Mukono (a town on the Kampala to Jinja road) to assess if the land was suitable for purchase to build a Bible school. We arranged to visit the land on the day before I was due to leave Uganda to fly to Britain. This was convenient, as I needed to spend a night in either Kampala or Entebbe due to an early morning flight. It was arranged for me to spend the night at Patrick's flat in Kampala.

On the day arranged, Okumu Wilberforce and I travelled to Kampala and we met Patrick at Kampala Taxi Park. After leaving my bag at Patrick's flat we met the lady who was selling the land and drove to Mukono to see it. When I met the lady I realised that I had met her on a previous occasion. On an earlier visit I had preached at the Makerere Apostles Church in Kampala, and the lady in charge of the church was the same lady who was selling the land. The lady's son-in-law had been Uganda's ambassador to the United Nations, and had spent some time in London as a diplomat.

The land was quite a long way outside of Mukono, along a red earth road and into the bush. Whilst driving along the road a long black snake slithered across the road in front of the car. This was the first snake I had seen in Africa, although I have seen a number of snakes since. On a later visit, whilst sitting on the veranda of Christine's house enjoying a bedtime hot drink, she told me that one of her dogs had been ill during the day. She thought that the dog might have been suffering from snakebite because a snake had been seen on the veranda earlier.

"What veranda?" I asked her.

"The veranda we are sat on now," Christine replied!

I spent the final night for this visit at Patrick's flat in Kampala and flew to Britain using Ethiopian Airlines the following day. There was no problem this time. I had confirmed my seat before I had even left Britain! If you remember, it was problems on the previous visit that had made this particular visit possible.

8.

ON TO MBALE

Mbale is Uganda's third largest town and is situated on the eastern side of the country, not far from the border with Kenya, and dominated by Mount Wanale. The town has grown due to the area being opened up to industry and modernisation, and is a good centre for reaching the towns in the northeast of Uganda. Mbale boasts a Roman Catholic cathedral and the Islamic University in Uganda.

Christine Birt moved to Mbale in 1993 to assist Living Water Ministries in pioneering a new work in the town. This new work was later to become an established church entirely in the hands of Africans and led by Okumu Wilberforce. Christine moved on to plant a church in the most rundown district of the town. When I first visited Mbale in 1995 Christine had already started the church plant by holding Sunday services in the main room of her home. There were already a large number of people attending and it was becoming obvious that premises were needed for a church building.

Note: a church plant has nothing to do with a palm tree in a large container, or a yellow tractor as seen on a building site. A church plant is when a new work is started, ideally in an area where there is no current Christian witness. The plant, that is, the new fellowship is nurtured, fed with

God's word and encouraged to take root and flourish into a church.

On this visit, Christine met me at Entebbe and the journey as far as Jinja was familiar. The taxi (minibus) was going through to Mbale, non-stop. The distance from Kampala was about 190 miles, or to put it another way, four hours by high-speed taxi!

The taxi we used was driven very fast, and very badly. I could see that Christine was struggling hard to keep her temper as the miles went by. Upon reaching Mbale Taxi Park somebody (not the driver) suggested that we should pay extra for my large suitcase. At this, Christine lost her temper and suggested that the driver should pay us for the way he was driving! The suitcase was carried free!

We took a private hire car to Christine's home and the fare was normally 2,500 shillings (at that time). Usually, the driver asked for five thousand shillings, hoping to get three thousand. This driver had heard the altercation with the taxi people, and was so intimidated that he asked for the correct fare!

The fellowship meeting in Christine's home was called the Church on the Rock, and the pastor was Richard Ebunyu, who came from a village called Dokolo, just outside of Otoboi on the Soroti to Lira road. Richard had farmland in the Soroti district which his wife, Josephine, maintained in his absence. Richard divided his time between the farm and the work in Mbale.

During my first visit to Mbale Richard went to spend some time on his land, and Christine took me to visit him. We travelled by a very overcrowded bus to Soroti, a distance of around eighty miles, over very rough red earth roads, and then changed to a taxi for a twenty-mile journey to Otoboi.

We then travelled by boda-boda (passenger-carrying bicycle, described earlier) to Richard's farmstead. Along a path we rode. It was no wider than the footpaths we use in Britain whilst walking through the woods. Christine was on the first boda and I was on the second. We travelled on through the bush. In places we passed by small patches of land that were being cultivated. The local people looked very surprised to see a European woman on a boda followed by a European man on a boda. Not the sort of thing they normally saw going by their land. As we travelled along I realised that I was seeing things and going places that tourists did not see or visit. I decided that it was much better to visit Africa on mission than as a tourist. I discovered, at the end of the journey, that we had travelled for six miles in this fashion!

Just as I was starting to think I was going to spend the rest of my life sat on a bicycle we suddenly entered a clearing that housed several buildings. We had reached Richard's home. I don't know if this hamlet had a name, but it has been known ever since as Richard's Place. There were a few mud huts and a couple of brick-built buildings. There were also a number of large brick mud receptacles with straw lids. They looked like the cooking pots you see in the old jungle films, only much larger. I expected to see Bob Hope's head suddenly pop out of one! I was told that they were used for storing grain. The receptacles stood on bricks to prevent rats from entering and spoiling the grain.

The mail had gone out to the district on the same taxi that we had used. Some years earlier I had been part of a dispatch unit in Britain for a Gospel broadsheet called *Soon*. This was an A4 paper, printed on both sides with testimonies in easy English (English especially for people who did not use it as their first language), and published by a British missionary society. The paper also offered a Bible course. Copies of *Soon* had been included in the mail delivery and people were to be seen reading them. It was good to see the receiving end of the process.

Christine and I spent two nights at Richard's Place. For our evening meal, the first evening, we were given chicken. We could tell that it was undercooked, so we ate as little as possible. There is a fine line between offending our hosts and using common sense. As the evening progressed I started to feel quite ill. There was a door at the back of the building in which we spent the night. The front door, the one we would use normally, was not accessible as people were sleeping in a room in between.

"There's the way out," Christine said, "if you feel ill during the night."

"Don't worry," I replied. "I've noted the emergency exit!"

After a good night's sleep, with no emergencies, I felt much better.

At breakfast, however, the same chicken meat was offered. When the chicken was presented again at lunchtime Christine decided that it was better to offend our hosts rather than be ill, so she told the people who were preparing the meal that we could not eat it because our stomachs were not as strong as theirs. She had taken a loaf of bread along (she had been in this situation before!) and somebody produced tomatoes. Whilst everybody else enjoyed chicken Christine and I enjoyed tomato sandwiches.

We both preached at the Otoboi Assembly and people received Christ as Saviour. There are nearly always a number of non-Christians at meetings in Africa, even at the meetings designed for church members. The church members invite them, or sometimes they just wander in to see what is happening. It makes me feel humbled as quite often, in Britain, we can find ourselves preaching to Christians only, even in evangelistic services.

At the start of the meeting, before the preaching, notices were given and leaders from the churches around the district greeted the visitors on behalf of their own fellowships. One man brought us greetings from the Muslim community!

Before returning to Mbale, one of the local church leaders brought a visitors' book for me to sign. I duly signed it, putting my name and address, and the man walked away. He had only moved a few steps when he suddenly stopped and turned around.

"Is Mansfield anywhere near Farnsfield?" he asked.

I could not believe what I had heard. Farnsfield is a small village in Nottinghamshire. Most Ugandans do not even know where a large town like Mansfield is, never mind a small village like Farnsfield. It would have made more sense if the man had asked if Mansfield was near Nottingham, which is a large city.

The man showed me the visitors' book and pointed to an address. There it was. Not only had the area had a visitor from Farnsfield the year previously, but also the visitor was somebody I knew.

9.

KILLER SNAKE RUNS RAMPAGE!

I spent Christmas 1997 in Uganda and flew to Entebbe with EgyptAir, changing at Cairo. A few weeks previous to the flight I had written to the London office of EgyptAir asking for an increase in weight allowance as I was visiting a missionary for Christmas and wanted to take some extra things. Permission was granted and I was advised to quote the name of a certain person as I checked in at Heathrow Airport.

I presented myself at EgyptAir's check-in desk, quoted the name I had been given, and the check-in girl's eyebrows shot somewhere to the top of her head! Not only was my extra-heavy suitcase accepted without question, but I was also pulled out of the queue and given preferential treatment all the way onto the aircraft!

There was no preferential treatment at Cairo. I thought that I had better not quote any more names. It was chaotic. EgyptAir flew good planes. The service on the aircraft was excellent. But Cairo Airport let them down. Considering that a jumbo had just landed from London and the airport management must have known that it was coming, there were hardly any staff on duty. It was the longest queue I had ever been in. I eventually made my way to the front. We were having our passports taken off us! I am very fond of my passport. It gets me back into Britain! To hand it over to somebody who does not look very organised takes a lot of faith. I asked the man how I would get my passport back. He pointed towards a door. As everybody else appeared to be going through the door, I joined them. I hoped that I was the only person who didn't know what he was doing. It turned out that nobody knew what they were doing! I don't think that even the staff knew what they were doing!

I went through the door and found myself in a large room full of check-in desks, just like any other airport. The big difference was the crowds of passengers milling around, wondering what they were supposed to do next. I found the check-in desk for Entebbe. There was a long queue. I could see a pile of passports on the desk. I hoped that mine was one of them.

To pass the time I decided to go into the little room marked Gents. I think that it was the Duke of Edinburgh who once said to go at every opportunity because you didn't know when you might get to go again. An attendant greeted me. He pointed to the urinals. Then he pointed to the washbasins. Then he handed me a paper towel and hit the button on the hand drier for me. Then he held out his hand. So I shook his hand and said, "Thank you." It pays to misunderstand sometimes.

I eventually retrieved my passport and made my way towards the gate for Entebbe. I was happy. The only thought that was clouding my mind was that I had to make the return journey two weeks later.

The turn of the year is the wet season in Uganda, and after meeting me at Entebbe, Christine Birt bought a newspaper from a vendor on a street corner in Kampala.

"Just look at this!" Christine exclaimed.

The headline read *Rains cut off Iganga highway*. The story told of a bridge being washed away by a swollen river just outside the town of Iganga. This is one of the most important roads in Uganda as it links Kampala and Jinja with the border with Kenya and onwards towards Nairobi and Mombasa, which is one of the main ports for East Africa. Traffic from the DR Congo also uses this road to reach Kenya. We needed to use the same road to reach Mbale. It did not bother me too much. After all, if a road was closed they simply diverted you, didn't they?

Another headline on one of the inside pages of the paper disturbed me more, for a short while. The headline read *Killer snake runs rampage*. I wanted to see where the snake was, to make sure it was not around Mbale. As I read the story I realised that the film Anaconda had been released on video, and that I was reading a review!

We drove on towards Jinja. We were using a private hire car. One of the advantages of using private hire was that the driver listened to the passengers, and drove at our speed and not his own. Another advantage was that we could stop for refreshments when we wanted, and not travel with parched throats gagging for a drink.

We passed by Jinja and headed towards Iganga. We were well on the way towards the town when we saw lorries and coaches parked at the side of the road. Quite a few of the vehicles had Kenyan or Congolese number plates. We had arrived at the washed-away bridge. We waited. Richard Ebunyu and the private hire driver walked towards the bridge to find out what was happening. It seemed an eternity before they returned.

"The soldiers are repairing the road," we were told.

"Can we wait?" asked Christine.

"We cannot wait."

"Why not?"

"It will take three days."

I suggested that there might be a diversion, and was told not to be silly. It was then I realised that to reach Mbale, we had to cross the river somewhere, and that this was the main road, Uganda's version of a motorway. If the bridge on this road had been washed away, then any bridges on any minor roads, if any minor roads existed, would be in an even worse state. I relaxed and settled back into my seat. I had two Africans and an experienced missionary with me. Why should I be worried?

There followed a couple of hours of discussions, which included phrases like "What do we do?", "We can't stop here all night.", "Where's the nearest shop?" (Actually, Iganga, with shops, wasn't too far away, but it was the other side of the river.)

A policeman walked along the middle of the road, saying to drivers, "You can go. Small vehicles only." We tentatively joined the procession of cars, vans, minibuses and pickup trucks, all moving slowly towards Iganga. We were moving. And we were moving in the right direction.

After a short distance along the road we turned left onto a very narrow red earth road, which ran through bushland. We were still going in the right direction, as we needed to turn left beyond Iganga to drive northeast towards Mbale. But we still had the river to cross. After a considerable distance we found ourselves in a traffic queue. We had come to the river crossing. We edged forward until it was our turn to cross the river. There was a minibus in front of us, full of people. The minibus slowly moved towards the edge of the ford, when all of a sudden, it dropped down! The roof of the bus was level with the road!

"Oh my goodness!" Christine exclaimed. "Can we do that?"

Our driver gingerly moved the car forward. We all held our breaths. We moved towards the edge of the swollen river. Men from a local village were guiding us, some holding on to the sides of the vehicle. Down we went, almost vertically. It was quite an experience. There is a Don Moen song with the lyric God will make a way where there seems to be no way, and I hummed it to myself. Through the river we went and out the other side. The road improved after this, and eventually we came across a main road that took us to Iganga. A welcome cup of tea in a café, and we were off again. We were back on the road to Mbale.

The journey had to be made again a few days later. Before leaving Britain a friend and I had taken boxes of medical supplies to a freight company in London to be air freighted to Entebbe. Richard Ebunyu and I went to Entebbe to clear the boxes and take them to Mbale. And, horrors! The road was blocked again! At the same bridge! This time, it was evening, and it was dark. I had visions of using the same diversion through the ford that we had used a few days earlier, but this time in the dark. After a long wait at the side of the road, the bridge was opened, and we were able to carry on, using the main road.

It was almost midnight by the time we reached Mbale and Christine, who had not been to Entebbe with us, was so worried that she couldn't eat her evening meal. When we had not arrived at her home at the time she expected us to arrive she had sent one of the boys who worked for her to the police station to ask if there was any problem. The boy had gone to the bus station instead, and was told that there had been an accident at the bridge and that some people had been killed. Christine wondered how she would tell my family back in Britain that I had been killed. If the boy had gone to the police station, as Christine had asked him to, he would have been told that no Europeans had been involved.

Christmas Day dawned. The extra items that EgyptAir had allowed me to carry included Christmas presents for Christine from her family and friends in Britain, and also a few birthday presents, as Boxing Day is her birthday. I managed to reach the dining room before she did and placed her presents where she would find them.

"What's this?" asked Christine, as she came for breakfast.

"Santa's been," I replied.

Walking to church on Christmas Day in shirtsleeves in a temperature of 29 degrees Celsius was another new experience. I had to remind myself what season we were in. Some of the houses were decorated with tinsel and Christmas songs sounded from cassette players. One song I heard was the Bing Crosby classic 'White Christmas'. It was surreal given the temperature.

The Christmas Day service was much the same as a

British Christmas Day service, except that the carols were sung in the normal lively African way. The Sunday school performed their nativity play, just like children all over the world. There was the youngest one who wondered why he was wearing a cardboard crown on his head. There were the angels who looked like fairies (why are angels always girls when the ones in the Bible have men's names?). There was the little boy who sang off-key. Whether you thought it delightful or disastrous depended upon whether they were your own children or not.

Normally, at Christmas, Christine's staff went to their families for a holiday, but one of Christine's house girls, Margaret, had volunteered to stay. Christmas dinner was a new experience for Margaret. Among the extra items I had taken were a packet of sage and onion stuffing, a trifle mix, a Christmas pudding, a jar of mincemeat and, yes, a box of crackers. Margaret was amazed. She had never seen such things. It was worth taking them just to see Margaret's face. She couldn't understand why Christine and I thought that the corny jokes in the crackers were funny. Margaret thought that they were, well, corny.

It reminded me of an incident with a different house girl some years earlier. Christine had decided to make a rice pudding. Usually, in Uganda, rice is boiled in water, so the girl looked amazed as Christine boiled the rice in milk. Then sugar was mixed with it. But the poor girl had to leave the room when it was served with jam. As far as she was concerned rice was served with meat and gravy.

I had heard Christmas dinner clucking in the yard the evening before. I decided that I was not even going to look at the chicken whilst it was still alive. During Christine's early years in Kamuli she stayed with a family until she had her own place. She had made friends with one of the chickens that were allowed to run loose. One day, she returned from ministry, and it was chicken for dinner. She was partway through eating it before she realised that her pet chicken wasn't around any longer.

10.

THE BUS RACE

It was time for my children to experience Africa, so in 1997, I took my son, Michael, and in 1999, I took my daughter, Christine.

It is interesting to be with people who are visiting a country for the first time. I like to put myself in their place and try to see things the way that they do. For both my children it was the first flight, and I cast my mind back to my first flight. I was quite pleased that both Michael and Christine acted as though boarding a plane was no different to boarding a bus. In fact, one of the highlights for Christine was drinking tea on a moving coach on the journey from Mansfield to Heathrow.

I sense the same interest and excitement when I meet people at airports who are visiting Britain for the first time. I have met a number of people in that way. I have tried to see things from their perspective on the journey to Mansfield.

Michael and I flew British Airways with a stop at Nairobi. Airports seem the same all over the world, but we were craning our necks to try and see a part of Kenya. We flew on to Entebbe and the heat hit us as we left the plane. We had to remind ourselves that it was February. It was so good to feel the hot sun after the long, cold British winter.

We cleared immigration and customs and Richard Ebunyu met us in the arrivals hall. The long journey to Mbale started. We travelled along the road to Kampala, Michael first looking at one side of the road, and then at the other. I pointed out some of the sights that I recognised. The Air France plane that the Israelis had rescued the hostages from, which had been turned into a museum. The guesthouse I had stayed at on previous visits; Entebbe Beach on the shore of Lake Victoria.

I was to repeat the process with Christine two years later. When I travelled into Kampala with Christine we found ourselves in the middle of a traffic jam. We saw a traffic policeman jumping around and waving a rifle.

I said to Christine, "Try not to laugh." A bus reversed towards the car we were in and only stopped when our driver reached out and banged on the back of the bus with his hand.

Kampala Taxi Park, with its hustle and bustle and chaos and confusion, was a similar experience for both Michael and Christine. We transferred to a taxi for Mbale. Hawkers were trying to sell us all manner of things whilst we waited for the taxi to fill. There were watches, biscuits, handkerchiefs, plastic bowls, clothes pegs, and ties. If it could be carried, it was being sold. The item we welcomed the most was the bottles of soda (Pepsi, Fanta and so on). We bought sodas.

We left Kampala and travelled towards Mbale. We drove on and on, on our four-hour journey. Out in the countryside we passed villages of mud hut houses, and they appeared to be more dilapidated the closer we travelled to Mbale. Michael wondered what sort of a house Christine

Birt lived in. He was rather relieved when he eventually saw it.

Christine, at this time, lived in quite a modern building in the Indian Quarters of Mbale, just a short walk from the town centre. There was running water, most of the time. During one of my visits there was a drought as there had been no rain for several months, and the water was available for only a few hours each day. When the rain eventually came floods washed the crops away, which created a famine. Electricity was available every second night. The power stations could not generate enough for demand, so it was rationed. There was a pattern, and if we were in darkness one evening, we could look forward to the lights being on the following evening. Frequent breakdowns brought extra power cuts.

By this time, the church that Christine had planted had moved out of her home and a bamboo cane structure had been built in Namatala. Namatala is the most run down and needy area of Mbale. At that time it was a haven for drug abusers, prostitutes, thieves, murderers, and all the lowest of the low. If anybody wanted to hide from the police then Namatala was the place. A person could disappear in Namatala, whether they intended to or not. And this is where the church was planted. We can praise God that the area has now improved, although there is still a great need for more improvement. As we walked through Namatala to the church building we could smell the stills used for making a strong alcoholic beer. This beer was very potent. It was drunk from a large pot and those participating sat around the pot with long straws. It was their social activity. There was nothing else to do in the evenings.

It is a well-attended church, mostly by people from the area. The local people were grateful that somebody had taken an interest in them. Some members of the church came from outside of the area as they saw the need for a Christian witness, and the church had thrived. Richard Ebunyu was pastor of the church in the early days and Christine remained the missionary up to the time of writing. The deacons are elected from the local people, making them feel that it is truly their church. The church seeks to minister to people's bodies as well as their souls, with medical help, help with employment and advice in all areas of life.

Christine at that time was President of the Mbale branch of Prison Fellowship International. She was responsible for arranging services and Bible study sessions in the prisons around the district. Christine was assisted by a good team of preachers and Bible teachers from churches of all denominations. She has since handed the leadership over to Mary Eteu, a local businesswoman, although she still makes regular visits into the prisons to preach and teach.

In the town there is the main prison, which is the largest prison in the area. At the side of the main prison there is the women's prison. Many of the women prisoners have babies with them. There are also a number of smaller prisons around the district. Prison is a mobile community, with new prisoners arriving all the time. The Gospel is constantly preached, and prisoners making commitments to Jesus are followed up with discipleship and Bible teaching. At one point every prisoner in the women's prison was born again. The authorities responsible for the prisons have let it be known that they are pleased with the work that Prison Fellowship International is doing, as the difference in the prisoners can be seen.

I introduced Michael to travelling by boda-boda, the passenger-carrying bicycles. We set off to travel from Christine's home to the centre of Mbale. We were in convoy. Christine in front, as she knew where we were going. I was second and Michael brought up the rear.

I told my driver to, "Follow the white lady with the sun shade," as Christine was carrying a large parasol. Very hard to miss – so I thought. We arrived at a roundabout in the centre of the town and Christine's bike turned towards the post office, which was to be our first port of call. My bike, followed by Michael's bike, turned along a different road towards the bus station. Most boda drivers don't speak English, and this one didn't. I tapped on the driver's shoulder to try and stop him, but that made him pedal harder. He probably thought that I had a bus to catch. I eventually managed to stop him, and we turned around, back to the roundabout, and along the road to the post office. I repeated that we wanted the white lady with the sunshade, but it meant nothing to my driver. The white lady with the sunshade was standing by the side of the road, and we shot by her. More tapping on the shoulder, and we eventually stopped once more.

This time, I got off the bike, told the driver to "Follow me", and we walked back to where Christine was patiently waiting for us to sort ourselves out. The driver of Michael's bike obediently followed us, wondering what these strange Europeans were doing.

Christine and I used bodas to visit the prison and, on one journey, at a junction, we parted company once more. You would think that two people who were obviously together, swapping bags and so on, would want to go to the same destination. But no, when we reached a junction Christine's bike turned left towards the prison and mine turned right towards the town. Again I tapped on the driver's shoulder. Again the driver pedalled faster. We eventually stopped and I tried to make the driver understand that I wanted to go to the prison. I was just thinking that the quickest way to get to the prison might be to hit a policeman when somebody who spoke both English and the local language came along and explained to the driver where I wanted to go. By the time I reached the prison Christine was inside and had started the service. She knew that I would turn up at some point.

On one boda journey my hat flew off. I tapped on the driver's shoulder to try and stop him and he pedalled faster. I'm not sure about this, and nobody has ever told me, but I think that tapping on a boda driver's shoulder is a signal to go faster.

Peter Clifton-Sprigg is a Bible teacher, and was the leader of a Bible school called Oasis of Life. When I visited Uganda with Michael in 1997 Peter was based in Lira, where a school was in progress. Michael and I paid a visit.

Lira is around 160 miles from Mbale and Michael and I travelled by bus. The first eighty miles to Soroti passed without incident. It was an enjoyable journey, and the road was not too bad. The bus was overcrowded, but that is expected in Africa. After a short stop at Soroti we set off for the second part of the journey. The road deteriorated as we left civilisation behind. As we journeyed along, a bus from a rival company dared to overtake us. The race was on. At times we were in front, and at times they were in front. For a lot of the time, we were side by side. What little traffic there was on the road pulled into the side to let us pass. The passengers on both buses were urging the drivers on, and we bounced and juddered over the potholes in the road. We pulled into a bus station in a small town. I don't know how the passengers on the other bus fared, but nobody got onto our bus, and the conductor pushed off the passengers who wanted to get off. Then the race was on again, until we reached Lira.

We spent an enjoyable few days with Peter and his wife Anne at the Bible school. The students had graduated from the first part of the school a few weeks earlier, but they had delayed the graduation ceremony, as they knew that visitors from Britain were coming. I felt very much honoured. I managed to embarrass myself by getting locked in the lavatory, and the door had to be broken down from the outside. Oh dear, what can the matter be?

In Uganda, everything is late. The public transport runs late. Church services don't start on time and definitely don't finish on time (there is no point in staring at your watch after one hour, hoping that the preacher takes the hint). If you are invited to stay for dinner you may as well cancel the rest of the day as dinner is probably still running around the back yard. So, it was a bit of a surprise when the private hire car arrived twenty minutes early.

It was time to travel back to Mbale, and Michael and I were to catch the six o'clock bus from Lira to Otoboi, where we were to break the journey by visiting Richard's Place. We had booked the private hire car for 5.30, expecting it to arrive any time in the half-hour after that. It was now 5.10, and there was an impatient driver honking his horn at the gate to Peter's Bible school. And there we were, in the middle of breakfast, and not a thing packed.

Michael and I hastily packed our bags, said quick goodbyes to the students who had gathered to see us off, and clambered into the car. We arrived at the bus stop by 5.30. The bus was there. It was due to leave at 6.00, and we thought that it was going to leave on time. It left at 8.00. We sat and waited, dreaming of the two hours extra we could have had in bed.

We broke the journey at Richard's Place, where we were shown around the estate. We called it the Ponderosa after an American television programme. Richard didn't know what it meant, but he liked the sound of the word. As we left to complete our journey to Mbale we were given a live cock chicken "for your dinner". The chicken sat between my feet on the bus from Soroti to Mbale, looking up at my face as though he was saying, "You are not going to eat me, are you?" I was in danger of turning vegetarian by the time I had reached Mbale.

11.

DRAMA IN UGANDA

Beginning of the Unheard (BOTU) was a drama group, which at that time, took a regular part in my ministry in Britain. For a number of years I had been urging the director, Eric Bexon, to make a visit to Uganda. Three members of BOTU, Eric, Michael (my son), and Matt Jamie, made a visit in February 2000.

My daughter, Christine, and I travelled out to Entebbe a week beforehand. Christine Birt met us, along with Marion Smith from Chesterfield. Marion was spending some time working with Christine Birt. I had already met Marion in Britain before she had flown out to Uganda. Christine (Birt) and Marion left Christine (my daughter) and me sitting in the airport restaurant whilst they visited the customs warehouse to try and release boxes of freight that had been shipped out from Britain a few months previously. After a few hours they had to give up as time was passing, the situation was getting complicated, Christine and Marion were aware that Christine (I'm sure you can work out which Christine is which) and I had flown overnight from Britain, and we still had to travel to Mbale.

By this time Christine had moved to the Senior Quarters district of Mbale. This is the area where most of the businesspeople and missionaries live. For the first time since living in Uganda, Christine had European neighbours. Senior Quarters is a pleasant area, a little further from the town centre than Indian Quarters, where Christine had her former home. There are large fields in the area, with footpaths. Just right for taking her dogs for a walk. It was interesting to see other Europeans taking their dogs for walks, too. It was similar to an English country park on a Sunday afternoon.

Christine, at that time, had four large dogs for protection. One of them, a big black dog, which was named Samson, had a mouth like a crocodile and teeth like elephant's tusks. At least, that was the impression I got the first time I saw Samson. Samson decided that I was his friend. I was very pleased about that. Another dog decided that I was not his friend. I wanted the chair he was lying on, as the light was good for reading. The dog vacated the seat, but snarled and snapped at me in such a way that my heart was thumping as I sat down. A few moments later the lights went out. This was an unexpected power cut, so we were not ready with torches and oil lamps. It was dark, very dark. And I was in a room with a dog that did not like me.

When light was restored Christine told me, "When you catch the dog's eye, tell him that he's a good boy."

I replied, "I want the dog to tell me that I'm a good boy!"

On an earlier visit, when Christine had just one dog, there was a commotion one morning at 3.30. I could hear a vehicle's horn honking and a man's voice calling, "Greta, Greta." I thought that the neighbours were having a 'domestic' incident, and tried to ignore it. But the call was insistent – "Greta, Greta" – and somebody was banging on what sounded like our gate. I heard Christine leave her room and stand outside the door to my room, and I quickly dressed and joined her. She was living in the Indian Quarters at the time, and a carpenters' workshop was part of the premises. A lorry had arrived to deliver timber. The driver was calling for Margaret, the house girl. At half past three in the morning my brain does not connect 'Greta' with 'Margaret', and Margaret didn't sleep on the premises anyway. As her family lived close by she went home each evening. Richard emerged from his room and took charge of the delivery. Christine and I had a cup of tea. We were both wide-awake by this time, and if we had tried to sleep, we would have heard timber being unloaded for the next hour. Where was the guard dog whilst all this was happening? Fast asleep on Christine's bed!

The time came to meet the members of BOTU who were coming, and Marion, Richard Ebunyu and I set off for Entebbe in a hired minibus driven by a man called Geoffrey. We had reached the outskirts of Jinja when the minibus rolled to a silent halt at the side of the road. Geoffrey jumped onto the back of a boda and went off to find a mechanic. Richard went to find sodas. Marion and I sat and waited.

After a while, Geoffrey returned with a mechanic, the vehicle was repaired, and off we went again. It was dark by the time we reached Kampala, and we drove through the city and on to Entebbe where we planned to spend the night at a guesthouse. As we had intended to reach Entebbe earlier in the day we had not booked any rooms, so we prayed that rooms would be available in the guesthouse we wanted to use, a guesthouse that I had used during a previous visit. Rooms were available.

The following morning we went to the airport to meet Eric, Michael and Matt. We arrived early and went into a café in the observation lounge on the top floor. Full English breakfasts were on the menu, so Marion and I took advantage and ordered one each. Full English breakfasts were few and far between in Uganda. Richard and Geoffrey ordered something else. There was plenty of time before the flight was due, so we thought that we would enjoy our breakfasts. We waited, and we waited. Then we waited some more. At one point we thought that we had been forgotten, so Richard enquired at the counter. No, we had not been forgotten. Breakfast was coming.

As we waited a South African Airways jumbo landed. Geoffrey and I, who were sat facing the observation window, saw it. We realised that it was the flight from Heathrow. We estimated that it would take the BOTU team around thirty minutes to clear immigration. Twenty-five minutes later, breakfast arrived. Richard asked for his breakfast to be put on a hot plate whilst he went to arrivals, on the ground floor, to meet the team and leave them in a café close by.

I ate my breakfast as quickly as I could, with all thoughts of enjoyment and savouring every mouthful gone, and went downstairs to meet Eric, Michael and Matt. We drank sodas and relaxed until the others came to us.

A number of us had business to conduct in Kampala, so we called into the city centre. As Eric and Matt wanted to phone home we visited the main post office where public telephones were situated. It was St Valentine's Day and a local charity was using the special romantic day to promote AIDS awareness. A group of girls in the post office handed out red roses and little packets. I won't tell you what was in the packets, but we 'lost' them and the roses were handed to Marion when we returned to the minibus.

We started the journey to Mbale. We stopped at Mukono for lunch at a café. We ordered our meals and settled down to wait. The power went off, making the long process even longer. We could smell the paraffin as the 'alternative' cooking equipment came into use. I told the lads, "Welcome to Uganda,"; a phrase they would hear a number of times a day during the coming week. When the meal arrived Marion thought that she could see teeth in the meat on her plate, but closer investigation revealed that it was bone.

Again, we set off for Mbale. We passed through the town of Lugazi and the van came to a standstill once more. Geoffrey managed to start the engine, but rather than take a risk, we turned back to Lugazi where we had noticed a filling station with a workshop. The man at the filling station directed us to a place that specialised in commercial vehicles and we spent the next few hours waiting for repairs to be completed.

Night had fallen by the time we reached Mbale, and we all wearily rolled out of the minibus to be greeted by Christine, some of the staff and the dogs. Supper was enjoyed, and my dream of having a drama team in Uganda was fulfilled.

The following week was filled with drama ministry in two of the local prisons, and in the church Christine Birt had planted, which by this time had been renamed Namatala Mustard Seed Church. We travelled around in the minibus, which had its own ministry of breaking down. On one journey, as we drove from Christine's home into town, the van broke down a number of times in a short distance. There was a young woman walking. We would pass her with the bus, and then break down. The young woman would then pass us. Then we would pass her again. This happened a number of times. We all laughed.

We used the minibus to travel to Lira, a distance of around 160 miles, and we managed to arrive without any breakdowns. On the way we called at Soroti, which is around halfway between Mbale and Lira. The company I worked for in Britain at that time had made contact with a prospective customer in Soroti, and we made a courtesy call. The customer was impressed.

After lunch in Soroti we travelled on to Lira where I interviewed a church leader on behalf of a Bible school student in Britain (another Christine!) who was studying cultural differences in evangelism for her thesis. We spent the night at a hotel, one I had used on a previous visit.

The following day the drama team were to minister at the Otoboi Assembly, just outside of Soroti. We set off for the journey. We were well into our journey when the minibus rolled to a silent halt at the side of the road. Yes, you guessed it – we had broken down. Geoffrey hitched a lift from a passing car and went in search of help. We settled down to wait. There was not a shop in sight so we could not have a drink. Eventually Geoffrey returned with a mechanic, the van was repaired, and we resumed our journey.

We turned off the main road and travelled along the narrow path which passed for a road to Richard's Place. At one point a very worried-looking small boy ran along the road in front of us before running off into the bush. I could just imagine the conversation when he arrived home.

"Mummy, I've just been chased by a van full of white people."

"Stop telling lies and eat your tea."

It was some hours later by the time we reached the Otoboi Assembly, but the congregation had waited for us. In Britain, we would have found the building locked and not a person in sight. But these people had waited for us. They knew that we were coming. They did not know where we were, but they knew that we were coming. And the programme was full. Nothing was omitted because we had started late.

We spent the night at a hotel in Soroti and returned to Mbale the following day without incident. A few days later and it was time for Christine (my daughter) and me to return to Britain, leaving Eric, Michael and Matt to spend a further week in Uganda, where they were a blessing to many, many people.

12.

DISAPPOINTMENT AT MANG'O

In 2002 I made a four-month visit to Uganda. This was the longest time I had spent in that country up to that time. It was beneficial as I was able to get to know the local people and develop closer relationships with them.

Christine Birt met me at Entebbe Airport, along with Sam Waniaye who was a Bible school degree student at this time, and was, at the same time, pastor of the church at Namatala, and Moses, who was a private hire driver. Moses became our regular driver when we needed a car, as we tended to phone for him if we were at home, or seek him out if we were in town. We knew his regular waiting place when he didn't have a passenger.

I had the privilege of attending the very first Sunday service of a church plant in the village of Mang'o. Mang'o is situated just outside of Mbale, on the side of Mount Wanale, which is part of the Mount Elgon National Park. The region is called Masaba Land and the local tribe, the Bugisu, worship the animist god Masaba by circumcising their young men as they reach adulthood. This is a very crude operation carried out by traditional 'doctors' whose only skill is obtained by actually doing the job. There was no church in the area and the few Christians who lived there travelled into Mbale to attend Sunday services.

Before the first Sunday service took place Christine led an evangelistic team in door-to-door work. Many people accepted the Lord Jesus Christ as Lord and Saviour and promised to attend services if a church was opened. A pastor was appointed to follow up these people and the church gained strength. They met in a schoolroom, which had been lent by the local headmaster.

A short while after opening the church a week-long evangelistic campaign was carried out with Pastor Okumu Wilberforce and a team from Living Water Ministries, who were based in Mbale. Door-to-door work was carried out during the daytime, led by Christine, and in the evening, Living Water Ministries held an open-air service. Many more people accepted Christ during the week, again with follow-up being carried out by the appointed pastor and his leadership team, some of whom were only new Christians themselves. During this week approximately one hundred people made commitments to Jesus.

The bad news is that the church has since collapsed, and all the work has come to nothing. We discovered that people were eager to become Christians only because the pastor had promised them that the mzungus, which means people with white skins, Christine and me, were going to pay to educate their children. This, of course, was wrong and put us in a difficult situation. It wasn't what we were there for.

This is one of the problems we face. I mention all the work undertaken before the church collapsed just to show the efforts missionaries sometimes put in for nothing. Mission work is not all laughter and joy. There is quite often heartbreak and tears. However, the Gospel was preached and we can pray that Jesus will propagate His Word in the hearts of the people involved.

Many of the people carrying out the work of evangelism come from Namatala and are mostly unemployed. There is no Jobseeker's Allowance in Uganda and the people struggle to feed themselves and their families, let alone find the money to finance a church plant. They are doing worthwhile work. Let us encourage them with our prayers. Please pray for God's provision for all the work carried out in His Name.

Please pray for strength and health for Christine and all other missionaries. I've seen Christine return from a meeting exhausted because she has walked or cycled, and she has given of herself whilst teaching. People who minister will know that there is a responsibility involved. A responsibility not to stray away from the truth that God has given. There is a responsibility to give God's Word, and not our own thoughts. Pray that Christine and others will be granted continued discernment as they seek to be true to the Word of God.

I found many changes during this visit. Having been to Uganda for numerous visits it didn't take me very long to walk around Mbale and remind myself where the different places were, like the post office, telephone office, banks and so on. Some places I never needed to know about on previous visits, like the electricity office and the water office, I soon found. On one occasion a church member who wanted to show me where she worked invited me into to a shop that I was passing.

Some new supermarkets had opened up, and one of them housed the internet café that I made full use of. I could check my Hotmail account and take a look at the BBC News. I could even find out how Mansfield Town Football Club was doing!

A new holiday resort complex had been opened, named the Mbale Resort Hotel. As well as a hotel and restaurant there was an open-air swimming pool. A very beautiful place which would have been expensive anywhere in Europe, but the prices were reasonable. Christine and I celebrated my birthday by having a meal there, and after the meal, we relaxed by the poolside where there was a bar. We ordered cups of tea. The waiter never batted an eyelid, but he had to walk a long distance to the restaurant to fetch the tea. I wondered how many mzungus (white people) ordered tea in the bar area!

Christine moved house whilst I was there. The landlord of the former house had sold it and the new owner wanted to occupy it himself. She found another house in the same district (Senior Quarters) and moved in; lock, stock, barrel, poultry and everything. The landlord of the new house and his two sons lived in the boys' quarters around the back of the house. We hired a security guard who kept watch during the night, and of course, he came with us. It was, and still is, necessary to have a security guard, as armed crime is rampant. The second night I was in Uganda, for this visit, armed robbers killed a lady in a property adjoining ours. There were many instances of people being killed in robberies during the four months I was there, and we quite often heard gunfire during the night.

On the first night in our new home, one of the landlord's sons stayed out all night visiting a disco. He came home at 5.00am and, rather than disturb people by rattling the gate, he decided to climb over the wall. Mistake! Our security guard had orders (from his superiors, and not from us!) to shoot anybody climbing over the wall. However, the security guard had been in the army and he hesitated to check for a weapon. When he couldn't see a weapon, he didn't fire. The young lad received a lecture from the security guard, followed by a lecture from his dad. He very quickly realised that the best way onto the property, no matter what the hour was, was through the gate, making sure that the security guard knew who he was! Christine was only pleased that we didn't wake up to find a body on the lawn and the grounds full of policemen!

We had real value for money from the security guard. When Christine and I went out for a meal in the evening, and had to walk home in the dark, the security guard at the restaurant radioed our security guard at home to let him know that we were leaving and on our way back. The other security guards in the properties in between picked up the message and gave our guard progress reports as we walked home. As we approached our gate it would open mysteriously to let us through. It was really good to know that the right people were watching us.

There is a downside to the political situation in the north of Uganda. A group of rebels calling themselves the Lord's Resistance Army are seeking to rule Uganda using the Ten Commandments. Unfortunately, the leader of this group, Joseph Kony, is not living under these rules in his own life. He has numerous wives and concubines and he takes young girls, barely in their teens, captive as concubines for his troops. They also capture young boys, brainwash them, and train them to be soldiers. These rebels were about 120 miles away from where Christine was at the time I was there for this visit, but later, in December 2003, they were quite close to Mbale and British Consul officials were watching the situation.

The atrocities carried out by the Lord's Resistance Army are so terrible that they are unbelievable to people in Britain. I will give you just two examples from the time that I was there in 2002, but there are many more.

There was a daily long-distance coach that ran from Kampala, the capital city, to the north of Uganda. Coaches on this run had been ambushed five times in five weeks, with passengers and drivers being killed and coaches burned out. During the final week I was there a driver was killed, and it was the second time that his coach had been ambushed.

The Lord's Resistance Army attacked villages, taking the residents captive, and on one occasion, some villagers were murdered, chopped into pieces and cooked in pots. The remaining captives were only saved from being forced to eat their neighbours by the arrival of Ugandan troops.

Pray over the situation with rebels and terrorists. New groups are constantly appearing on the scene. Pray for the president of Uganda, Yoweri Museveni. Mr Museveni's wife, Janet, is a practising Christian, and whilst I was in the country for this visit, she led prayer meetings specifically to pray over the situation in the north. There are also Christians in the government. Pray that the good example of the president's wife and the Christian politicians continue to influence the president and his policies. But most of all, pray that the Lord Jesus Christ may be glorified in Uganda.

13.

IT'S THE DAY WE REMEMBER FOOLS

On 1st February 2007 I left Mansfield to make a twelve-month visit to Uganda. I looked forward to my longest ever visit to that country. In 2002 I had made a four-month visit, but this was to be for twelve months. Before I left Mansfield a friend suggested that the in-flight movie might be *Snakes on a Plane*. I'm pleased to report that it wasn't!

The power was off as I arrived at Christine Birt's home in Mbale at 9.30pm on 2nd February. The night had been spent at Dubai, which wasn't as glamorous as it sounds as I had kipped down on the airport floor. Being in the dark, in a home I hadn't been in before, left me a little disorientated, but the following morning, when daylight came, I was able to unpack my bags and sort my room out the way I wanted it. A walk around town in the afternoon brought me back into 'Mbale mode'. Some things had changed, but many things had remained the same, and I looked forward to seeing the church at Namatala.

We were, in fact, experiencing twelve-hour power cuts, usually from 8.00pm to 8.00am every second night. The power generating company said it was because the level of the River Nile was low. This situation never improved during the twelve months I was there.

The church building at Namatala at this time had brick

walls and an iron roof rather than the mud brick walls and straw roof it had in 2002. A building for the Sunday school was in the process of being built in the same manner, and a generous gift from Britain boosted the building tremendously. As I walked through the Namatala area it struck me how it was slowly changing for the better. Some of the rundown dwellings had gone and more sturdily built houses had replaced them. New shops were also being built. It was good to see these changes. There is still a lot of poverty in the area. It can become overwhelming at times.

Pastor Sam Waniaye took me to visit a church plant at Namabasa. The church building consisted of cane walls and a corrugated iron roof. It was a quarter of the planned size. The church started when Steve Jesney, from Louth in Lincolnshire, evangelised in the village the previous November. The church building felt peaceful, and the Presence of God was very strong.

Philip Lotimong, who had been saved through the ministry of the church in Namatala and had matured as a Christian, was pastor of the church at Namabasa. One Saturday morning a few months into my visit, I joined a group of people who had gathered at the banks of the River Namatala to watch as Pastors Sam and Philip baptised more than twenty people. Most of those being baptised had made decisions for Jesus during the crusade the previous November when the church at Namabasa was planted. Sam had the pleasurable experience of baptising both his mother and his stepmother.

Christine Birt was in New Zealand visiting family for the first couple of weeks I was there, and Sam Waniaye, Osika

Wilbert, who worked for Christine at this time, and I travelled to Entebbe Airport to meet her on her return. It was good to see Christine, and she was looking very fit and well. Before returning to Mbale we paid a visit to Entebbe Zoo and saw the animals there. A lion came to the wire fence of his compound to investigate us. We moved well back in case he decided to mark his territory in our direction. The only previous time I had visited this zoo was in 1990 when there was little more than a few snakes. The zoo has improved and is well worth a visit for those in the area.

On the outskirts of Mbale is a place called Salem, which is quite peaceful. There is reasonably priced accommodation for guests in little houses, with spacious bedrooms and en-suite bathrooms. Christine, Sam and I spent the day there discussing things in general and planning ministry. It was planned for me to minister in a different church each Sunday. The first Sunday in the month I would minister at Luseke, Sironko District; second Bukimuga, Bukonde District; third Namabasa and fourth Namatala. I looked forward to this.

Namatala was the first ministry for me and I spoke on the Glory of God. One man went forward for salvation even as the service was starting. This was very encouraging. A visit to Namabasa a few days later reminded me of the frustrations of working in Uganda. Things had gone so well, so far, that I had almost forgotten. Firstly, the car Christine had booked to take us to Namabasa was late arriving, then secondly, the interpreter went missing. The good, peaceful fellowship we shared with the people of Namabasa more than made up for the difficulties.

Luseke village, Sironko District, proved difficult to reach. Sam and I had to abandon the car two miles from the village as the road was too muddy, and there hadn't been any rain! We walked along a track and branched off onto a narrow path. We walked through long grass, trying not to think about snakes too much. The fellowship was good and I preached on the Armour of God, taken from Ephesians chapter 6. The whole church shared a fellowship meal after the service. We had goat meat, posho and cabbage. Brown beans and rice were also available. The church had been started by a man called Moses after he'd been saved from a life of drugs and drink at the church in Namatala.

One Sunday I was out of bed early to travel to Luseke. When I checked my diary I discovered that the date was 1st April, so I changed my calendar and checked again. It was All Fools' Day. I decided against mentioning All Fools' Day, as I didn't think that people in a small village in the African bush would know what I was talking about. I checked my diary again and discovered it was also Palm Sunday. Palm Sunday! It had completely missed me.

I heard God say, "Now that you know, you are going to change your message, aren't you?"

My first reaction was to say, "Aaaaargh!" My second reaction was to pray, and God gave me Matthew chapter 21, verses 1 to 11, which, upon checking, was an obvious passage.

When I asked at Luseke church if anybody knew which special Sunday it was, one lady answered, "It's the day we remember fools!"

On one visit to Luseke I went with Tom, Pastor Sam's

brother. Tom hadn't been before and was relying on my knowing the way. I'd been a number of times by now, so of course I knew the way! I missed a turning somewhere. We took a long walk through a swamp where I could hear frogs croaking. Where there are frogs, there are usually snakes. I tried to think of something else.

Bukimuga isn't strictly a church plant. Pastor Margaret, who was the founder of the church, felt the need of oversight for accountability, and asked if Bukimuga could become part of the group. Bukimuga is a village on the side of Mount Wanale, which is a mountain that dominates Mbale. Pastor Margaret started this church in her home village after meeting Jesus whilst working in Mombasa. There was no Christian witness in Bukimuga before this church.

To reach Bukimuga we travelled by car to the village of Namachele, which is also on the side of Mount Wanale. I could feel my ears pop on the journey upwards, like in an aeroplane. Then we walked for a mile or so along difficult paths to the village. At one point the path was quite narrow, with a cliff face on one side, and a long drop, which looked miles down, on the other side. This was quite difficult after rain, which appeared to be most times I went. However, we were rewarded with amazing views over Mbale. I don't know how many miles we could see, but it appeared to be a long way.

On a couple of Sundays Pastor Margaret and I went to Bukimuga in a four-wheel drive double cabin pickup truck belonging to, and driven by, Johnson, who was a deacon at Chrisco Church in Mbale. This vehicle took us along a different route, and on the first occasion managed to take us over rough roads with plenty of mud to just outside the village, when it was defeated by the final hill. The church was only a ten-minute walk away, so I consider that very good considering the conditions.

Part of the vehicle route uses a road, which is only just wide enough for one vehicle and has a cliff face on one side and a drop into a ravine on the other. On the second occasion, after a particularly heavy rainstorm, this stretch of road was slippery with mud. The vehicle, even with four-wheel drive engaged, was slipping and sliding, first towards the cliff face, and then towards the ravine. I could see that Johnson was struggling to keep us on the straight and narrow (Okay, not so straight, but it was narrow!). On future visits to Bukimuga I decided that it would be safer to walk using the original route.

Bukimuga is Margaret's home village, and is a heavy Muslim area. Several members of Margaret's family are Muslims.

Not only did I preach at Namabasa, the church plant, one Sunday each month, but I also taught on Friday afternoons. At the end of one teaching a woman I didn't remember seeing before came and knelt on the floor in front of me. I looked at the woman, and the woman looked at me. I thought to myself, *Be careful here, David. This might be a marriage proposal.*

I turned to the interpreter, and he spoke to the woman. She answered him, and an exchange of words started between the two. I stood between them, turning from one to the other, like watching a tennis match. I hadn't got a clue what they were talking about.

Eventually, the interpreter turned to me, and said, "She wants to be saved." I was amazed. I hadn't been preaching a Gospel message. I'd been teaching on prayer. There is power in God's word, and it never goes to waste. It appears that she had no intention of attending the meeting. She had never been inside the building before. She was passing by, and somebody had gone out and invited her in.

One Friday, when I arrived at Namabasa to teach I discovered that the bamboo walls had been taken down, and that brick walls were being built. So I taught with builders working quietly around me. I resisted the temptation to make a joke about foxes knocking walls down (Nehemiah chapter 4, verse 3)! I hadn't got far into my teaching when a torrential rainstorm started. As the walls were only around waist-high it meant that the rain came into the church building, wetting everybody and everything inside. I had the unusual (for me) experience of getting wet through as I taught and watched my teaching notes disintegrate in front of me!

The following Friday, back at Namabasa, the bamboo walls were back in place above the waist-high brick walls. There was a space at the top, in between the bamboo walls and the corrugated iron roof. There was another torrential downpour, and again, my teaching notes disintegrated in front of me!

One Wednesday evening, in March, whilst Christine and I were eating our tea during a storm, there was a loud crack of thunder, which startled us both. Then the power went off, and it was off for eight days. No lights, fans not working, fridge, freezer, TV, cooker, kettle and the mobile phones died one by one as they couldn't be recharged. How much we depend upon electricity. It transpired that a transformer had been put out of action by the storm and another one had to be brought from Kampala, then installed and tested.

A plumber visited the house on one occasion to fix a problem with the hot water. He was with us for two days, made a mess with water all over the floor, and left us in a worse situation than when he started. When Christine asked him where he had learned his trade he proudly answered that he was self-taught!

One Friday morning I met with Mary Eteu, who was the co-ordinator for Prison Fellowship International in Mbale, and an Australian lady named Carina, and we made our way to the women's prison. For my ministry I affirmed the prisoners as women using Proverbs chapter 31. Three of the girls made decisions for Jesus. Carina prayed for those who were expecting to appear in court during the coming week. The prisoners wore a blue smock dress and the officers wore khaki uniform, so I wondered who the lady was who was sat with the prisoners, and wearing civilian clothing. Perhaps she was a social worker? I discovered she was an opposition politician who was in prison for debt. She had demanded a recount at a recent election, lost the recount, but couldn't afford to pay the cost of it. I wondered where her supporters were when she needed them.

During one week I was struck, as I walked around Mbale, by the number of disabled people there were around.

Some had shrivelled arms and legs, and walked with crutches. Others had no legs at all and moved around on their stumps, propelling themselves with their arms. It was heart-wrenching to see them. There seemed to be more than usual on Fridays, and when I mentioned it at home it was pointed out to me that Friday was the Muslim holy day and it was the duty of Muslims to give to those in need. The Muslim shopkeepers gave the disabled people money.

Walking home from town one day there had been an accident between a taxi (minibus) and a saloon car. There didn't appear to be any injuries, but both vehicles were battered. The standard of driving in Uganda is quite bad, with right of way rules being ignored. The boda-boda cycles are especially bad as they weave around without any indication of where they are going, pulling out across the front of motor vehicles without warning. I found it heart-stopping when I was the front seat passenger in a car, and it kept me alert the few times I drove.

The motorcycles in Uganda are interesting to see. There can be three or four people on them. It is not unusual to see a dad up front, with a toddler in front of him sat on the petrol tank, and mum sat side-saddle behind with a baby on her lap. None of them would be wearing crash helmets. Sometimes there are three adults, one up front and two riding pillion. Not a crash helmet in sight. Women generally ride side-saddle, even when riding three up.

During one visit to town I decided to have a haircut. There was already a customer in the chair, so I went to sit in the waiting area. The hairdresser waved me to his other chair, and I sat in it. He then abandoned the customer he already had, gave him a newspaper to read, and dealt with me! The customer accepted it without question. In retrospect I should have insisted that the first man be dealt with before me, but surprise had caught me out.

14.

I WANT YOU TO BE MY FRIEND

During June 2007 Christine Birt found another house to move into. The place we were at that time had a hostel either side of it. The hostel on one side had small children who were very noisy until late in the evening. They were unsupervised, and somehow knew Christine's name and kept on calling to her. The hostel on the other side had teenage girls (I dubbed them St Trinians) who were up and about, active and very vocal, at 5.00am. I tried to imagine British teenage girls being up and lively at 5.00am!

On the day we moved to our new home I awoke to a pleasant surprise. I could hear praise and worship coming from the girls' hostel next door. I grabbed my torch and looked at my watch, and it was 5.10am! We knew that there was a group of Christians in the hostel as we had heard them worshipping some evenings, but it was the first time I had heard them in the morning. On my final morning in that home, for the first time, I enjoyed being woken by the girls next door!

The house Christine found to move into was close to the former home, but on a much quieter street. There was a large ground area for animals and poultry to the rear, and a garden to the front. Great improvements all round.

Whilst we were still in the former house we spent three days over one weekend without running water. There was a large tank in the compound, which held enough water to see us through the regular cut-offs, but in this instance the tank ran dry and eighteen jerry cans of water had to be bought on Sunday afternoon. We didn't know when the water would be restored, as the water company, like the power company, do not explain what the problem is, or the likely timescale. When we had the eight-day power cut mentioned in the previous chapter, the power company, when phoned, denied there was any problem for the first three days.

One Friday evening, as Christine and I were relaxing before going to bed, we felt the house shake. Christine called out, "Earthquake!" and, as it was raining outside, she grabbed an umbrella and I grabbed my torch and hat, and we ran outside. We called Julie, one of the orphans who stayed in the boys' quarters, who joined us. The other orphan, Egitu, was at an overnight prayer meeting at Namatala church. It was at this point we realised that we had forgotten Hellen, a school secretary who stayed with us. I went back to the house to call Hellen just as she was coming out. Hellen was wet through, with her clothes sticking to her. She had been taking a shower when she felt the tremor, and had dressed without bothering to dry herself off! There were no further tremors, so we went back indoors. It all makes life interesting.

After one Friday meeting at Namabasa Pastor Sam Waniaye took me to see a nursery and primary school that was being built with the help of a group of supporters in Britain. Most of the walls had been built up to ceiling level, but the floor, roof and fittings still needed to be completed. Three classrooms were planned, a head teacher's room, a staff room and a secretary's room. The building was surrounded by a large area of ground with plenty of room for expansion.

Pastor Sam then took me to see a house that was being built for Maria, the sister of Pius. Pius was one of the workers at the house, and a church leader at Namatala. Maria and her children were to live at one end of the house, and Pius, with his wife and children, at the other end. In the middle was planned a shared living room and kitchen. The builders were actually working on the house whilst we were there. This house was being built with the help of another group of supporters.

Christine, Pastor Sam and I paid a visit to Salem, which is a mission complex on the edge of Mbale. As well as a guest house there is a hospital, which was being upgraded to carry out major operations, clinic, workshops (tailoring and carpentry), school, orphanage, driving school and nursery (plants). There may be other projects which I have forgotten about. Various people and organisations were supporting the different projects. It was impressive.

As I was walking along Republic Street in Mbale one morning a young woman wearing a short skirt came alongside of me. After a while she said, "Hello."

So I replied, "Hello."

Then she said, "I want you to be my friend."

I looked at her out of the corner of my eye and thought to myself, I don't particularly want to make friends with a young woman wearing a short skirt.

Then she told me that she had seen me in church, so I asked, "Which church?"

She replied, "That church," which as far as I was concerned, might have been anywhere.

After a series of questions I managed to discover which church she had seen me in. Then she told me that she wanted me to give her two thousand shillings.

Another young lady, who was operating a telephone kiosk, called me over and told me that she wanted me to be her father. I told her that I already had two daughters, natural daughters, in Britain.

"Oh," she said. "You have another one now."

One Monday through to Wednesday, to comply with Visa regulations, I visited Busia, Kenya. I stayed at the Blue York Hotel, which I found very comfortable, and spent most of the time reading and praying. I had a good walk around the town on the Tuesday and found the one and only internet café. At one point I was walking through what I thought was a lorry park when I saw a gate and a building that looked familiar. It was the border back into Uganda! I did a quick about-turn. Close to the hotel there was a shop with the name Armlice Chemists. My armpits itched each time I walked by it.

On the Wednesday I returned to Uganda and was met at the border by Pastors Sam and Philip. We had a meal in a café at Tororo where we saw, on CNN TV, Gordon Brown having his first Question Time as Prime Minister. I returned to Mbale to find that the power had been off since the previous day. Welcome home! The power was back the same evening.

The following Saturday I discovered that a large amount of money had been taken from my room during the previous day, and I was quite upset. The bedrooms were right inside the house, and the money was well hidden, so somebody we had been trusting had taken it, somebody who had had the time to go through my belongings. As we hadn't been in the house very long, and there was extra work to do, there were people around who were not normally around, but who were known by either the landlord or ourselves.

The following day I preached at Bukimuga, but I was still upset and I almost cancelled. There was a special anointing whilst preaching, for which I was grateful and able to praise God. God is at His strongest when we are at our weakest.

28th July saw my birthday, and some of the church leaders, and their wives, came to the house for a meal. It was so good to share my special day with special people. We ended the evening by standing in a circle on the front lawn to sing worship songs.

As everywhere else most weeks in Uganda are a mixture of good events and bad events. The difficulties seem more pronounced when we are far from home, in a culture which isn't our own. I'm sure that any missionary in any developing country would say the same. One typical week started with having to cancel my ministry on the Sunday. The money taken earlier in the month had finally caught up with me and I couldn't afford the transport costs. This was extra ministry arranged for me at Shanzou, which is another village on the side of Mount Wanale. I felt very bad about this, as I don't like cancelling arranged ministry.

The following day, Monday, one of the staff, Pius, was reaching for a bow and a number of arrows, which had been put on the garage roof when we moved into the house. Loose bricks fell and hit Pius on the head. We gave him first aid treatment, the best we could, but he declined hospital treatment. Pius was back at work the following day, boasting about his head being thick!

Tuesday, and the old dog belonging to Christine, Babu, was sick with tick fever. A vet gave Babu two injections, one of which was very painful. Babu died shortly before I returned to Britain.

On the upside there was a beautiful heifer calf born during the week, which was accepted by the other cattle. A bull calf had been born a few months earlier.

The week just described was not exceptional. These sorts of things are happening all the time. If missionaries don't mention them it's probably because they are used to them. Please pray over daily life for missionaries. Difficulties abound right across the developing world.

On the Friday of the week described above Christine and I travelled to Kampala as my Visa was expiring on the Saturday and needed to be renewed. The immigration officer told me I could have a special pass and gave me an application form. I was asked to take it back the following week.

When Christine pointed out that my Visa was about to expire, the immigration officer said that it was "no big deal"! So I became an illegal immigrant for a while.

Pastor Sam and I travelled to Kampala the following week to hand in my application form for the special pass. We were told that the application would take seven working days to process.

When Christine and I had travelled to Kampala the previous week there had been an accident on the Jinja to Kampala road involving a petrol tanker, which had tipped over into a ditch. A crowd of people surrounded the tanker with jerry cans, collecting the petrol which was pouring from the tank. We could smell petrol very strongly, and it would only have needed a moment's carelessness, perhaps with a cigarette or a spark from a passing vehicle, for there to have been an inferno. The tanker had been recovered by the time Sam and I travelled the following week. Please pray for safety for missionaries as they travel around. At that time it took four hours to travel from Mbale to Kampala. Today the journey is longer time-wise, due to the increase in traffic.

Sam and I made a further journey to Kampala a few weeks later expecting to collect my special pass, and I was told that I needed a work permit. Thus started the long process of collecting the required documents, including a criminal record report from the UK.

When it was pointed out that my Visa had expired I was told, "Don't worry about it."

Christine travelled to the UK at the beginning of September for a four-week visit. Whilst Christine was away we started to hear reports of heavy rains in the Karamoja District, which is in the northeast of Uganda. People had been killed, mud hut houses, crops and bridges destroyed, and roads made impassable. Heavy rain was forecast for eastern Uganda until December. There had been no dry season during the year and very few crops had been harvested, as they had been too wet. Food shortages were expected. Africa is at the mercy of the weather. Too little rain, and the crops don't grow. Too much rain, and the crops are destroyed as they are either washed away or rot in the ground. Imported food is expensive and only the rich can buy it.

Later into September, and much of the north and east of Uganda had been declared a state of emergency by the government because of the flooding. There was a wide band of disaster across Africa stretching from the west coast to the east, including Uganda. Osika, one of the staff at the house, visited his family in a village in Soroti District one weekend and found himself stranded. He experienced continual rain and had to wade through floods that were waist-deep. As Osika returned to Mbale on the Monday the vehicle he was travelling in was stuck in mud four times. A bridge over a river just outside of Soroti was flooded and in danger of being washed away. Osika could see fish swimming over the bridge! There were areas in the north of Uganda in much worse condition, and which could only be reached by air. The UN brought in a helicopter from Sudan, and was trying to find two more. When we consider the size of the disaster, not only in Africa but in Asia too, we can appreciate the task that the governments, UN and aid agencies were facing. Because of the flooding there was a high risk of disease, including cholera, and mosquitoes were breeding to epidemic levels. We really needed God's mercy.

Storms were experienced in Mbale over three afternoons. There was a power cut at 2.30pm on the

Wednesday afternoon, and I had just finished preparing my teaching for the following Friday. The teaching needed printing off the computer, and I couldn't do it! Remembering that a storm-induced power cut once lasted eight days, I stared at the printer in disbelief. The computer itself had a backup battery, so I was able to save my work. When we realised that the power cut was only affecting three or four houses I decided to phone the electricity supply company to make sure that the engineers knew about it. A machine with a female voice answered the phone and offered me options. *Aaaaargh! I thought I'd left those behind in Britain!* Somebody must have known, however, as the power was restored in the middle of the following morning.

On the Friday afternoon the rain was so heavy that I thought the River Nile had diverted its course and was running through the front garden!

As I walked to Bukimuga one Sunday morning somebody said to me, "It's the dry season now. It's only the rain that's making it wet!"

The end of September arrived, and it was time for Christine to return from her visit to Britain. On the day before Christine was due to return Jim and Norma Gregory, and their son-in-law, Ty, arrived for a two-week visit. Jim and Norma were pastors of the Church on the Rock in Leamington Spa, and Pastor Sam and I travelled to Entebbe Airport to meet them.

After spending the night in Kampala we all returned to Entebbe to meet Christine, and we started the long journey to Mbale.

As we stood at traffic lights in Kampala there was a sudden loud bang at the side of us. A minibus taxi had failed to stop, and hit the back of another minibus taxi, which was second in line at the lights. This taxi was then shunted into the back of a further minibus taxi, which was first in line. The taxi at the back then hit the taxi second in line for a second time. This made the second taxi hit the front one a further time. This all happened in the lane on the left side of us. The windows in the taxis shattered, and passengers leaped through the windows to escape. A young boy, perhaps around ten years old, was crossing the road in between the second and first taxis, and he was squashed. A look of intense pain came to his face as he fell to the ground.

Somebody shouted, "He's dead," and as the police waved us by we could see the boy's lifeless body lying on the road. Please pray for any missionaries you know as they travel around. In many developing countries there is a relaxed attitude to bad driving and poor vehicle maintenance.

As Pastor Sam and I travelled to meet Christine and the others we followed a minibus taxi with chickens tied upside down to the roof. We appeared to follow this mobile torture chamber for mile upon mile through the outskirts of Kampala. There is a great need for education regarding animal husbandry, and most animals are treated cruelly. It is quite upsetting to see and the locals make a joke out of it. It is down to attitude. There are people in Uganda who seek to uplift the country and improve life for all, but they are fighting against attitude all the time.

Pastor Sam Waniaye took me to visit an elderly lady

at Namabasa who had a swollen stomach. Food poisoning was suspected, but the lady herself thought witchcraft might have been the cause. The lady was responsible for two grandchildren who had been orphaned. There is a lot of need in these villages. Medical treatment has to be paid for in Uganda, and villagers cannot afford it. No medical access means misdiagnosis. Food poisoning, malaria and flu cover more serious illnesses which don't get treated. The church tries to help, the missionaries try to help, but funds are limited.

The lady died the following week. She had been an active member of Namabasa Church, most Sundays giving a testimony of God's goodness in her life and singing a song to Him.

There is a background of witchcraft and superstition at Namabasa, as in most African villages. On a number of occasions demons manifested during the worship time and were dealt with. We can expect a reaction when Jesus is worshipped with passion.

A relative of Osika Wilbert, one of the staff working in the house, died in Kampala. She was an eighteen-year-old girl who had kidney trouble. The family failed to raise sponsorship to take the girl to India for treatment.

Almost every week there are appeals in the Ugandan newspapers for sponsorship to send people to India for major operations, most notably heart surgery. Major operations are almost unavailable in Uganda, although a hospital in Kampala is making advances in some areas, including heart surgery. People are dying through lack of facilities that are readily available in the developed world.

In the UK, and I am sure in other countries too,

there are people retiring from paid work who have high qualifications, and a good number of years gaining experience and skills. Some have paid into pension schemes and have been able to retire early and receive comfortable incomes. Many of these people do not want to live inactive lives; they want to use the qualifications, experience and skills they have gained in the voluntary sector. I would make a plea for those with medical skills to consider using those skills in the developing world. Of course, my particular plea would be for the Mbale region of Uganda, which would touch a wide area full of need, but the rest of Africa, and other developing continents, are needy too. The need is not exclusive to the medical sector, but also with maintenance, engineering, administration, business skills and so on. There is more about this in the appendix at the end of the book.

15.

IN THE BLEAK MIDWINTER

On one visit to Entebbe I spent an hour or so at Entebbe Beach whilst Pastor Sam Waniaye was elsewhere. There was a café at Entebbe Beach, which offered the choice of chicken and chips, or fish and chips. I ordered fish and chips, and settled down to drink a Coke and read a newspaper. The fish and chips were served. Now, I wasn't expecting Bridlington-style fish and chips, but neither was I expecting what came to the table. The chips were okay, so was the salad, but the fish was a complete fish: head with eyes, skin with scales, and tail with fins. My knife and fork hovered over it, but a wide-open eye was looking at me! I ate the chips and salad, but tried to ignore the fish. Today, many years later, I like to think that I would take a deep breath and eat it. Experience brings willingness to try different things – I think!

I had an experience with an ostrich one Friday. As I walked along the street we lived on, on the way to town, I saw the ostrich at the end of the street. It looked as though it was going in the opposite direction to the way I wanted to go. I passed the big bird, and walked on. After a few moments I heard a clip-clop, clip-clop, and the ostrich ran by me, followed by a Land Rover with a worried-looking driver, who edged his way past the bird. By this time the great feathered thing was walking alongside me.

I wondered how tame this creature was. I noticed that the Africans were giving it a wide berth, so I thought that I'd better do likewise. The ostrich had large feet, like one of those clowns we see at the circus, and had plenty of meat on its thighs. I wouldn't have liked to be on the receiving end of a kick. It decided to turn onto a side road, across the front of me. I thought it prudent to give it right of way.

Whilst Jim Gregory, from Leamington Spa, was visiting Pastor Sam was ordained as senior pastor of Namatala Mustard Seed Church. Sam had actually been senior pastor for some time, but was now officially recognised. He earned his degree the previous year and wore his graduation gown and mortarboard cap for the ceremony. After being ordained Sam then ordained Osika Wilbert as assistant pastor of Namatala, and the pastors of the other three churches in the group, Philip Lotimong (Namabasa), Margaret (Bukimuga) and Peter (Luseke). Jim and Norma, and their son-in-law Ty, then returned to Leamington Spa.

All four of the church buildings in the group needed a lot of work to make them permanent. Namatala Church was the most established, but the building still needed renovation work to bring it up to a modern standard. It needed connecting to the electricity and water services. Namabasa Church building was being constructed as funds allowed. As I returned to Britain Steve Jesney was working hard on it. Bukimuga Church had a brick building, but it was too small. When I visited I usually found it crowded. A larger building was needed. Luseke Church, at this time, met in a borrowed building. The owner of the building was happy, but the owner's family were complaining. They now had their own building. The churches needed to meet in their own permanent buildings to let the local people know that they were there to stay.

Christine Birt had to cancel ministry in Bungoma, Kenya in October due to lack of funds. Pastor Sam went alone by public transport to keep costs down. The cost of ministry is high, especially if there is a need to spend time away from home. There are transport costs, a Visa if going into Kenya (Sam doesn't need a Visa as he is an East African national), hotel costs, and we are expected to contribute towards the costs of the conference such as feeding and accommodating the delegates. Most, if not all, delegates to a conference came from poor backgrounds and often spent all the money they had simply travelling there. A lot of them needed help returning home! We wanted to bless these people with good quality teaching, but it costs.

In my own ministry I noticed the cost of transport increasing after petrol price rises. This was the beginning of the large-scale worldwide increases that plagued the first half of 2008. The cost of a private hire car to Namabasa increased by 50% in the space of a few weeks. Transport became so expensive that, in the final few months before returning to Britain, I walked the two miles or so to Namabasa. Normally, two miles are nothing to me, but the sun was often beating down as hot as 35 degrees Celsius. There was a two-mile walk, followed by a meeting lasting for two or two and a half hours under a corrugated iron roof, followed by the return two-mile walk. Walking through Namatala on the way home I had to stagger into a pub for a Coke. I felt like one of those cowboys we see in

Western films staggering into a saloon bar after walking across the Arizona Desert!

Alwyn and Mary Griffiths from South Wales paid a visit to Mbale and Christine and I met up with them. Alwyn and Mary were running a school at Bunabutye, near Sironko. Although the school was now open the building work continued and the presence of the school was uplifting the area.

Steve Jesney from Louth in Lincolnshire arrived in November. Steve was the person who held the crusade at Namabasa in 2006 when the church was planted. He had brought with him a braille Bible for a blind member of Namatala Church, James Opio, whom Steve had met on his previous visit. As Steve entered the church building James was leading worship, and Steve held him in a bear hug. I could see from the expression on James' face that he hadn't got a clue who was hugging him!

Sam and I again travelled to Kampala to submit my work permit application. There had been a delay due to waiting for a criminal record report from Nottinghamshire Police, and I was concerned that it might cause a problem. It was a shock to be asked for a document that I hadn't been asked for previously, but a visit to another office cleared matters up. Ten working days had to pass before the permit would be issued.

Another visit to Kampala; the work permit had been approved and we paid for it. Then we were told the permit would be ready in three days after it had been processed! We were advised that anybody could collect the permit, as long as they had the receipt. Sam collected it a few days later as he visited Kampala for another reason.

We had taken Stephen, who lived at Namabasa, to Kampala with us. Stephen was an older man who did some small jobs around Christine's home. He hadn't visited Kampala since he was five years old, and he was amazed at some of the things he saw. We had to explain to him how the cars reached the top levels of multi-storey car parks. All he could see was the cars through the gaps. We used a lift at a shopping centre, little thinking that Stephen hadn't seen one before. He obediently followed us into a little room, the doors closed, there was a slight shaking feeling, the doors opened, and the shops were different!

During December we heard the disturbing news that Ebola was spreading rapidly through western and northern Uganda. Ebola is highly infectious, being passed on through body fluids, including sweat. President Museveni issued a press statement advising people not to shake hands, as hands were likely to be sweaty in the hot weather. The president said that a simple wave of the hand was better. This proved to be difficult as church leaders, along with business and professional people, automatically shake hands.

It was rumoured that there were a number of cases of Ebola in Mbale Main Hospital. This proved to be a false alarm. A lady who had recently visited the infected area died in the hospital due to, as it turned out, pregnancy complications, which is another issue in Uganda. It was correct for the authorities to take precautions, and it made the people of Mbale aware of how serious Ebola is. It was reported that, as the virus passes from person to person, it loses strength, until it fades out altogether.

Christmas in Uganda is different from Christmas in the UK. On Christmas Eve a group of us visited Tororo to see the apes in the forest. A main road passes through the forest and the apes gather around the edge of the road as people throw food to them. This is something we don't see in Sherwood Forest! We followed this with a meal at the Rock Classic Hotel in Tororo town.

As we returned to Mbale we called at a market where Christine bought cabbages, onions, cooking oil and a few other things, and we delivered them to Mbale Main Prison to go with a cow that the prisoners were to eat for Christmas dinner.

In the evening, back home, we had a visit from Sheila, a missionary nurse from Devon. After a meal we sang carols on the veranda by candlelight and moonlight as there was a beautiful full moon. We opened with my favourite, 'In the Bleak Midwinter'. The temperature in the daytime was 30 degrees Celsius!

On Christmas Day Christine and I went to Namatala Church where Christine preached on 'The Word Became Flesh' (John chapter 1, verses 1 to 3, and verse 14). At the end of the service Pastor Sam announced that the church was fasting from Boxing Day until New Year's Day. I tried to imagine a British minister making a similar announcement!

After church we visited the village of Aloyet, which is Hellen's home village. Hellen was a school secretary who lived at the house with Christine. She spent Christmas with her family at Aloyet.

Travelling to the village was a nightmare. We had booked a car with one of our regular drivers, who told us he was coming. He actually sent another driver, who appeared with a car with no handbrake and no seatbelts. This driver then proceeded to take us into town so that he could change his tyres. The vehicle was obviously unfit for the road, even by Ugandan standards, so Christine found another driver who agreed a price to take us. Partway into the journey the driver received a phone call from the car's owner to say he wasn't charging enough money. The driver took us back into Mbale, where we found a third driver and car, agreed a price with him, and he took us.

The good news out of all this is that Hellen's sister-in-law, Grace, made a decision for Jesus during our visit to Aloyet.

As January arrived news came of violence and killings in Kenya due to a dispute over election results. Thirty people had been locked in a church in Eldoret and burned to death. Eldoret is a town I visited in 1990 when I was with Youth with a Mission (YWAM). Uganda is a landlocked country, and imports via sea use Mombasa docks and travel across Kenya to the border. This route became dangerous and a number of lorries with Ugandan number plates had been set on fire. This resulted in a shortage of fuel as tankers used the same route and the drivers, understandably, refused to bring them. The little fuel available became expensive. After a few days the tankers resumed their journeys with army escorts.

The time came for me to leave Uganda for this visit, and it was a time of saying goodbye. At Luseke, Sironko District, I was given a chicken at the end of my final meeting. It isn't good to give names to anything we are going to eat. Henrietta went down a real treat a few days later.

At Namabasa we shared a meal before the final meeting. It was good to enjoy fellowship with these people I had come to love. God is blessing His church in Uganda. God is blessing the work of missionaries and the national church leaders. But there is a price to pay. There is the price of hard work. A lot of the days are just hard slog. There is the repetition of routine. There is the struggle to discern God's message when ministering. There is the stress of dealing with rules and regulations that are constantly changing.

For missionaries there is the price of misunderstanding. The culture is different. Little misunderstandings, which go unchecked, lead to major problems. It happens in Britain. Imagine the confusion when there is a cross-cultural misunderstanding.

However, the results are good. The Gospel is preached. The lost are saved. The sick are healed, and demons are cast out. I've heard testimonies from people who I trust of the dead being raised to life.

If there is anybody reading this who is feeling God's calling to the mission field – and please don't think that you are too young or too old – if anybody is feeling God's calling, then make sure that it is from God and not simply your own feelings. You need God's calling, and God's anointing, to survive. But if it is God's calling, then go for it. You will see things you have never seen before. You will visit places you didn't even know existed. But the result will be the thrill of being obedient to God.

May Jesus Christ be glorified in each of our lives, wherever we are.

16.

(This chapter is based on a sermon preached at various churches after a visit to Uganda made during January and February 2010.)

CARING THROUGH PRAYER
PHILIPPIANS CHAPTER 1, VERSES 3 TO 11

How much are we caring for the people we pray for? Do we receive a prayer request, pray over the request, and then get on with our lives? Or do we ask God if we can do anything about whatever we are praying for?

Or do we pray for people, but forget to let them know we are praying for them? It is easy to say, "I'll pray," to somebody, and then walk away and forget, or simply give a quick prayer, and then forget to follow it up. I know; I've done it.

I've been making regular visits to Uganda since 1990, where I preach in village churches in the Mbale District, which is in the east of Uganda, not far from the border with Kenya. During my latest visit to Uganda in January and February 2010 I preached twice at Luseke Church. Luseke isn't a village as such. It's more a collection of homesteads. It's around six miles from the nearest main road, deep in the bush, with no proper road to reach it. The vehicle we travel in has to push its way through the growth. It is snake-infested with cobras, mambas and other species.

At the end of the service after I had preached at Luseke the first time, I turned my mobile phone on, and found a text message. It was from somebody from my own church in Mansfield, and it contained the single word 'Praying'. It was so encouraging! The lady who sent the text didn't realise that I would be surrounded by snakes when I received it!

Don't forget to pray for those overseas, and don't forget to let them know. I was grateful for the messages of encouragement I received via text and email.

Caring through prayer. The best way to care for people is to pray for them. Prayer leads to action. Quite often, as we pray for the people we care for, or the situations on our minds, God drops into our minds the action that He wants us to take.

The second time I preached at Luseke, on my final Sunday for this visit, two young men made decisions for Jesus. It made the journey and the snakes worthwhile. I have a fear of snakes and I was very much aware that the area was snake-infested.

When I returned to Mbale from Luseke, I found that Christine had had her bag stolen on the way to the church she was due to preach at. The bag contained two Bibles, three cash cards, money, a mobile phone and spectacles. You can imagine that Christine was very upset, and it took away the joy of seeing two young men come to salvation.

I returned to Britain leaving Christine in that situation. The cash cards were the biggest problem. Banks in Britain issued two of them, and it was a major problem for Christine getting them replaced.

Care for your missionaries by praying for them. Many missionaries receive their money from Britain and stand the risk of being without money should their cash cards be stolen, or if there is a problem with the banking system, as there was when I was in Uganda.

Mbale has a number of ATMs with Visa symbols. These worked when first installed but, in 2010, were no longer working, except for one, which only worked at night – sometimes! I left Christine in that situation, and later communication with her told me that the situation remained the same for several months.

These are some of the practical problems they face daily, but we seldom hear of.

Christine took me to visit Peter Losiru. His surname translates as 'Mosquito'. Peter had been found on a rubbish tip early last year and had been left to die by his family. Church members found him and told Christine about him. Christine found accommodation for Peter and paid for his treatment. He was then much better, although one of his feet was in danger of being amputated due to infection.

Whilst we were with Peter we met his landlady. Her name was Sinima, and she was a Muslim lady who made Jewish skullcaps! Think about that for a moment! The skullcaps were beautifully made, decorated with the United States flag, the Ugandan flag and the Israeli flag. In the centre, where the seams came together, was the Star of David. Sinima also knew the Gospel story and was happy to talk about Jesus. We prayed that she would come to know Him as her personal Saviour.

Whilst in Uganda I visited various projects run by other organisations.

Steve Jesney, a missionary from Lincolnshire, took me to visit a school for orphans. Steve and a local pastor were encouraging the people who run the school to help themselves, using the resources they had.

Bricks were being made, using charcoal-fired ovens, to use in their own building work, with the surplus being sold to raise funds. Steve, who was a builder by trade, said that the bricks were of high quality.

We can care for people in developing countries by praying for them and encouraging them to help themselves.

One morning Steve took me to see a Rural Development Centre on the outskirts of Mbale. This was a vocational training centre run by the Church Missionary Society and Church Army. It was extensive. We saw animal enclosures containing rabbits, goats, chickens and a fish farm. There were plots of land growing various vegetables, and agricultural lectures were being given in rooms as we passed by.

Again, people being encouraged to help themselves, this time with better farming methods.

Not all the projects we visited were successful. Steve and I visited a project started a few years earlier. There was a restaurant, now closed, a church building, which was rented out to another group, and a partly-built Bible school. The project fell to pieces when the missionary was taken ill and had to return to the UK. It was now a sad area of neglect – an abandoned dream.

Please pray for good backup for projects, that people

may be trained up to take over should the missionary need to leave. Pray that sending churches take their responsibilities seriously. We can ask God if there are any lessons that we need to learn.

From that project Steve and I went to the Mbale Resort Hotel to see the new hotel being built on the already up-and-running complex. It was impressive! We went from a failed Christian project to a successful secular project! A good hour was spent sat by the swimming pool simply enjoying the surroundings.

We can care for missionaries by praying for their safety. There was a by-election in Mbale one day for a new MP. There was a lot of violence and that night gunshots were heard.

I heard of two deaths, and there may have been more. The following morning I walked into town wondering if I was doing the right thing. All was peaceful. Things were back to normal.

Pray for the safety of missionaries finding themselves in situations that happen suddenly. Violence can flare up without warning. Then peace resumes, again suddenly, and things are back to normal, as though nothing happened. Remember the World Cup in 2010? Bombs exploded in Kampala, Uganda's capital, as people watched the final.

The major upside of mission work is the love shown to us by the people we minister to. I had the privilege of speaking on Christine's radio programme on three occasions during this visit. During the final broadcast, just before returning home, I mentioned that Christine's bag had been stolen, and all the problems it was causing. A newspaper vendor, who was a regular listener, told Christine the following day that his daughter had burst into tears at the news. This young lady had never met Christine, she had only heard her voice on the radio, and yet she felt an attachment to her.

Mission work might be hard slog, with a lot of the work repetitive and mundane, working in difficult situations with power cuts, water cuts, phone and internet systems not working, cash machines not working, poverty everywhere we turn, people dying because they don't have the money for medical treatment.

But it's worth it to see people come to Christ. Christine saw twenty-two prisoners make decisions for Jesus during the time I was there. I preached five times in four churches and spoke at a conference one Saturday, and was uplifted by the love shown to me by the people. It is the people we meet, and become friends with, who make it all worthwhile.

It takes a special calling from God to be a missionary. There are those who go, see what things are like, and return home, distressed. Others go, see how things are, and stay, because they know, without doubt, that God wants them there. If you believe God is calling you to be a missionary, make sure that it is God's calling, and that you have His anointing.

Is God calling you to serve Him in this country, perhaps through your local church? If you are born again, then the answer is quite likely, "Yes."

Do you want to be effective for Jesus? Do you want to

see the people around you change because they see Christ in you? Are you willing to give up the sin in your life?

God blesses obedience. He does not bless disobedience. He does not bless those with sin in their lives.

What is sin? Sin is anything that prevents God being effective in a person's life. Sin is anything that interferes with our walk with Jesus.

If there is sin in our lives, and we know about it, then we need to deal with it. It may be an activity we do. The activity itself might not be harmful, but it may be interfering with our walk with God. It may be a relationship we are in, or it may be all sorts of other things.

God will point out, to each of us personally, those things that need dealing with. Please note that I am including myself. I constantly need to examine the things I am doing, and the people I am getting close to. It's a constant battle. We cannot afford to relax. We cannot afford to think that we have 'made it', to think that sin cannot touch us anymore.

There is a song written by Donna Lasit. Part of the lyrics say, "I say on Sunday how much I want revival, but then by Monday I can't even find my Bible. Where's the power, the power of the Cross in my life?" (Believe, City Bible Music 1999.) If we want to see the power of the Cross in our lives, then we need to be serious with God. Caring for others through prayer, and being prepared to be the answer to our own prayers. God blesses obedience.

17.

THREE MEN ON A MOTORBIKE

(This chapter is based on journal entries I made during a visit to Uganda in June and July 2013.)

UGANDA REPORT, JUNE – JULY 2013

The British Airways flight to Uganda was direct and non-stop, landing at Entebbe Airport on a Friday morning. At Entebbe I was met by Christine Birt and the driver, Moses. On Friday evening we arrived in Mbale.

On Sunday morning Steve Jesney, another missionary, arrived with his vehicle at Christine's home, where I was staying, to take me to Namatala Church, where I preached on Psalm 139. My aim was to let the people of these churches know that they were special to God. Sam Waniaye, the overseer of the group of churches, interpreted for me, and after the service, we arranged to meet the following day to discuss the programme and other logistics regarding the Leadership teaching.

Sam visited the following day, as promised, and we discussed the programme for the teaching, and arranged for me to visit Luseke Church, Sironko District, on the following weekend. Luseke is a small settlement way off the beaten track. There are swamps nearby, and a good selection of snakes. I try not to think about the snakes too much.

Luseke was a new church plant when I first visited in 2007, and I had been visiting since the early days. I always looked forward to being there again, but more about this later.

On Wednesday 12th June, I visited Mbale Main Prison with Christine Birt, where I had the privilege of preaching. I preached on Philippians chapter 4, verses 10 to 20: being content with what we have and trusting God to provide our needs. One prisoner came forward for salvation after Christine made an appeal.

The following Saturday Steve Jesney arrived with a local church member named Fred Masakala, who was to interpret for me, and we set off for Luseke Church. As we travelled along the road to Sironko something happened to the drive on Steve's automatic vehicle and we came to a stop. That evening I discovered that the timing had snapped and that the engine was ruined.

Steve told Fred and me to continue our journey whilst he sorted out his vehicle, and we used a minibus taxi to Sironko, where we changed onto a motorcycle boda-boda, called a picky-picky. There were three of us on the picky-picky: the driver, myself in the middle, and Fred. Three men on one motorcycle! This is something I thought I'd never do.

The picky-picky took us to Luseke Church where I delivered the Leadership teaching to forty leaders from local churches. It seemed to have been appreciated. Luseke is the church where I first received the vision for good Leadership teaching in 2007.

In 2007 I made a twelve-month visit to Uganda, and the main thing I noticed was that the Africans were good at evangelising. They didn't need evangelists. I also noticed that there were some good Bible teachers, but they tended to be in the larger towns. What I felt God impressing upon me was that good Leadership teaching was needed in the village churches, where the leaders couldn't easily travel into the larger towns, for various reasons including lack of finance for travel costs.

Since 2007 I have been researching Leadership teaching and I settled upon a course called Equip Leadership, which had been put together by Leadership expert John Maxwell. Friends who pray with me agreed this course was suitable. The purpose of this visit was to test it out with the leaders I want to reach.

The following morning, Sunday 16th June, Sam Waniaye collected me with a double-cabin pickup truck and we once again travelled to Luseke Church where I preached on Psalm 139. After the service we moved onto the banks of the River Sironko and saw eighteen people baptised. Seven were scheduled to be baptised, but eleven more made decisions for Christ and were baptised there and then. What a wonderful thing to see!

Whilst in Uganda I liked to visit other projects to see what other people were doing, and one morning Christine took me to see a farm started by a man named Jerome. The farm was called Dutch Farm, as Jerome was Dutch.

Dutch Farm was impressive, with European-style cattle pens for feeding and milking. Jerome made Gouda cheese and yogurt to be sold in retail outlets, and supplied milk locally. He was also starting to breed chickens to build up a flock.

Jerome had planted a small forest, and replanted trees to replace those he cut down for firewood. The cow manure was processed into methane gas for cooking in the home he shared with his wife, Petwa, and their children. On site there were a number of holiday-let chalets.

Local people were employed on the farm and there was potential for development. Good, proper employment was one of the needs for local people, and there were good opportunities for those with the skills in this area.

The following Saturday, 22nd June, Pastor Sam Waniaye and I travelled to Bukimuga Church, Bukonde District, where I presented the Leadership teaching. It was important to me that Sam was there as he was the overseer of the group of churches and I wanted him to assess the teaching. Sam enjoyed the teaching and said it was exactly appropriate.

My original intention for presenting the teaching in future was to use a CD-ROM with words on a screen for the participants to fill in the blanks on worksheets. Because of the difficulty with electricity my thoughts then went on to using a flip chart. However, Sam said that we needed to cater for those who were illiterate and suggested that I continue to present the teaching in exactly the same way that I presented it this time, that is, straight talks with handouts for the participants to take home and read. This I was happy to do.

One Sunday evening Christine and I went to Top Radio for the broadcast she made every Sunday evening. The following morning, Julius Hande, one of the men who worked at Christine's place, told me that the testimony I gave during the broadcast had encouraged him to continue to pray for the people close to him, even though he wasn't seeing the results. I was richly blessed.

Another Wednesday, and another visit to prison where I preached on Psalm 139. Christine prayed for the prisoners and made an appeal. Four prisoners came forward for salvation. It was a privilege to be there. After the service had ended Christine and I were taken to visit the sick bay, and on to the workshop where a number of the prisoners were making baskets and furniture. These were of excellent quality, and some of Christine's furniture had been made by prisoners. The standard was professional and the furniture wouldn't look out of place in any quality British furniture store.

Saturday 29th June was the best Leadership teaching day of the three I conducted. It was at Namabasa, but instead of taking place in the church, it was held in a school. There were around two dozen of us, and as we were sat in individual chairs, we were able to sit in a circle. Not only was this better for teaching but it also meant that I could sit down. It made for a more relaxed style of teaching. This is the way I want to present it in future.

The following morning I was back at Namabasa, this time at the church to preach on Psalm 139. My preaching was well received, and it was good to return once more to a church I'd been visiting since its early days.

Monday and Tuesday of my final week for this visit were spent catching up with emails and so on. On the Wednesday Christine Birt and I went to Mbale Main Prison where Christine preached, after which we went to the Pearl Haven Christian Centre to meet with their director, Okumu Wilberforce. Okumu and I first met in 1991 when he was assistant pastor at Kamuli Miracle Centre. He took us to lunch at Mount Elgon Hotel where we enjoyed beautiful fillet steaks.

The following Friday, 5th July, I flew to Heathrow and returned to my home in Mansfield.

18.

A FRIGHT IN THE NIGHT

(This chapter is based on journal entries I made during my visit to Uganda in March and April 2014.)

The lightning flashed, the thunder roared and the rain was torrential! Somewhere in the mountains a radio transmitting station took a battering, putting the radio station in the nearby town off air.

No, the above isn't the opening of a novel. It's the gist of the message Christine Birt and I received one Sunday afternoon a few hours before heading to the radio station for Christine's weekly broadcast.

The main reason for my visit to Uganda on this occasion was to present Equip Leadership training, and on the first Saturday Sam Waniaye, the overseer of the work, took me to present the teaching at Luseke, Sironko District. Most of the journey there was good as the roads were tarmacked, although full of potholes! The final few miles, though, were over unmade roads and full of mud. Sam drove very carefully, with the final half-mile or so being the worst stretch. At one point there was an explosion as the car lurched forward, and when we checked, we found a blown tyre. In fact, the tyre was ruined as there was a large tear in it. Sam replaced the tyre with the spare he carried and we were on our way. The return journey was easier as five hours of hot sun had dried the road somewhat, but Sam still had to drive carefully at certain points.

The Equip Leadership teaching was well received, with the dozen or so participants promising to pass the teaching on to others. As I was presenting the teaching the thought came to me that this is what it's all about. All the preparation work, and the training days at Stoke-on-Trent, were coming together as I passed the teaching on to these church leaders.

The Equip Leadership teaching again went well on the second Saturday, this time at Bukimuga Church, Bukonde District. Bukimuga village is on the side of Mount Wanale, and is quite difficult to reach by road, especially after rain. However, the weather had been kind over preceding days and the road was passable. Parts of the road, however, were quite close to the edge of long drops down the side of the mountain. One slip wouldn't have been very good for either car or occupants!

On the return journey, as we reached Mbale, we drove through a crowd of police and soldiers who had gathered outside the police station. Later I heard that a politician had been to town and that there had been a riot. We had driven through the aftermath! One of Christine Birt's workers, Julius Hande, happened to be in town and had received tear gas in his eyes. Everyone gets caught in a riot whether they intend to be involved or not.

The third Saturday, and I presented the final (for this visit) session of Equip Leadership teaching, this time at Namatala Church for the leaders from Namatala and Namabasa. Again the teaching was appreciated, and again the leaders present promised to pass the teaching on to the churches in other villages, some being in remote areas. The day before returning to the UK Philip Lotimong, the senior pastor at Namabasa, sent me a message through Christine to say that he was going to Kenya that day to teach leaders, and that he intended to use the teaching notes I had left with him as his basis for his teaching. A few weeks later, back in the UK, I received an email from Philip, which I reproduce below:

> *Hi David, Praise the Lord. Hope you are having a lovely Easter holiday. Thank you so much for the knowledge you passed on to me with that leadership equipping training. It is a really powerful tool. I had successful leadership training in Kenya. I was using the very notes. I want to tell you that people were so much blessed and encouraged. I had a team of 22 Pastors and Leaders. Pastors promised to extend it to their local churches. I am booked into one of the churches already in August for leadership equipping. Next month I will be travelling to Pallisa for Leadership training. And for all this I will be using the very tool. Please God bless you so much for your coming.*

Can you imagine how encouraged I am feeling? This is what it's all about!

On the first Sunday evening Christine took me for her broadcast at Top Radio where I had the privilege of giving a Thought for the Day type of short talk. My message was based on 'making a start'. The hardest part of any task, or project, is to actually make a start. We can research and research and research, until research becomes the main project, and the true project, the goal, gets lost.

The second Sunday, and we again broadcasted from Top Radio but on the third Sunday there was a torrential rainstorm which took the station off air. In May 2014 I received an email from Christine saying that the radio station was still off air. One of the things that happen in Uganda.

Whilst in Uganda I preached on two Sundays, at Luseke and Namabasa, and three times in Mbale Main Prison, seeing four men make decisions to follow Jesus. There is a thriving church inside prison and the men appreciate it when visitors give them time. It is such a privilege to feel a part of this church, which is a part of the worldwide fellowship of believers. The members of the prison church are our brothers. Please pray for them.

There are frequent power cuts in Uganda, and one night I went to bed during a power cut which lasted all night. In the early hours of the morning, whilst I lay awake in the pitch dark thinking what an ideal time it was for any intruders, my bedroom door burst open.

"Hello?" I called out. There was silence. "Who's there?" More silence. I felt for my torch, which was on the floor by my bed, and it took a while to find it in the dark. When I had located my torch I discovered that the door was ajar. When I checked in the corridor I discovered two dogs, with their heads cast down, but with eyes looking up at me; the classic guilty look that dogs have! It was a real 'fright in the night'!

One day in May 2014 I received an email from Christine Birt saying that Steve Jesney was on his way to the UK to have a brain tumour removed. Whilst I was in Uganda in March and April Steve collapsed in Christine's compound and we knew that he had some sort of problem. Clare Spencer, who lives in Mansfield but at that time worshipped at a church in Ollerton, was Facebook friends with Steve (as well as myself), and I sent her a Facebook message to let her know what was happening. I suggested to Clare that perhaps we could visit Steve when he was stable and we knew where he was. Clare sent a message back saying that it would be good to visit Steve when it could be arranged.

After a while I made contact with Steve via telephone, and he was pleased to hear from me. Steve brought me up to date with all that was happening with him, and I put it into an email which I sent out to a few people in Uganda. The email is reproduced below. I told Steve that Clare and I were planning to visit him, and he said he was looking forward to it. The email follows.

Just spoken with Steve on the phone and his spirits are high and he knows he is being well looked after. He's in Queensbury Hospital, but he's expecting to be transferred to Hull. Medical staff from both hospitals are meeting via computer link today to decide what to do with him.

It appears that the tumour near Steve's brain is making him suffer epileptic fits, but medication is reducing the tumour and he's feeling much better.

Clare (Spencer) and I are planning to visit Steve the week after next, and he's looking forward to it. I will phone him again in a couple of days.

Steve is grateful for all the prayers that are being offered for him. Please continue to pray that God will be glorified in all this, and for skill for the medical staff, and peace in Steve's heart. Please share this news with all who love and care for him.

Just prior to being discharged from hospital Steve said that he would probably go to Louth, where his mother and brother lived, although there might be a chance of staying with church friends in Grimsby. The day before visiting Steve, in June 2014, I woke up with the thought in my mind that I would rather go to Grimsby instead of Louth, as I knew my way to Grimsby. When I phoned Steve Jesney later in the day he asked me if I could go to Grimsby instead of Louth! *Yes! Of course I can!* On the following day Clare Spencer and I travelled to Grimsby, reaching the address Steve had given me at 11.00am, which was the time I expected to arrive. We found Steve quite cheerful, taking good care of himself, spending his days being looked after by his friend Jo McCabe, and his nights sleeping at Jo's dad's home.

Clare and I spent a lovely day with Steve and Jo, and we left around 4.00pm, I think.

Sunday evening, 6th July 2014, saw the start of a drama which lasted several days. At 6pm I was due to preach at Sutton Christian Fellowship in Sutton-in-Ashfield, and at 5.30pm, I went to my car to drive to the church building. The car would not start; not a glimmer! A message was showing on the dash in front of me – Airbag Failure. It was a "What?!" moment. At 5.40pm, after attempting to start the car a number of times, I realised that I had better phone for a taxi if I wanted to fulfil my preaching engagement, which I did, reaching the church just four minutes late.

On the following day, Monday, I had arranged with Clare Spencer to travel to Louth for our second visit to see Steve Jesney, who was in the Elms Care Home whilst waiting for an operation to have the brain tumour removed. I realised that I would need to hire a car for this, and on Monday morning, I sent a text to Clare to explain what had happened and phoned a car hire company. The car hire company said they were expecting a car back in at any moment, and that it should be ready by just after 10.00am, if I wanted it. I booked the car, sent a further text to Clare to bring her up to date and phoned Steve to explain that Clare and I would be later than arranged.

When I collected Clare I reached for my satnav to set it for the postcode of the care home we were visiting, and looked for the socket to connect the satnav. Clare and I searched the front of the car diligently, but neither of us could find the socket for the satnav. As it happened, I had printed a route off the internet, so we followed the route, occasionally continuing to look for the satnav socket. Neither Clare nor I could believe that there wasn't one.

Clare and I reached Louth, following the route without any problems, until we were half a mile or so from the care home. As we couldn't see the Elms Care Home anywhere on the road it was supposed to be on we asked a number of people. Nobody had heard of the Elms Care Home, including the receptionist at another care home! Then we saw a postman. Salvation! A postman always knows the local area like the back of his hand.

The postman blinked a couple of times, then said, "It's my first day on this walk." This was too much for Clare and me, and we burst out laughing. The postman asked us if we realised that the road continued on across a bisecting road. This is where the problem was. We were turning around too early. We found the Elms Care Home, and we found Steve.

Steve was looking well, and I noticed that his cheeks were more filled-out than I remember them being in Uganda, indicating that his appetite was good. He was being well looked after and was quite content where he was whilst awaiting his operation on 15th July. His spirits were high and Clare and I had a good time with him, laughing and joking.

Clare and I set off for home, following the reverse route I had printed off the internet without any problems. On the outskirts of Lincoln we called at a Tesco to use their café. When we returned to the car my eyes immediately rested upon the satnav connection socket!

"Look at that," I said to Clare, and we both stared at the socket. When we saw it, it was so obvious that neither of us could work out why we couldn't see it before. There is something in the Bible about having eyes but not seeing!

On the return journey to Mansfield I realised that, if I had been alone during all the happenings that day, it would have been a nightmare. Because Clare was with me, what could have been a nightmare turned into a day of fun. We had found the situation so funny that we simply laughed our way through it. It is so good to have a companion when we go through life's trials, tribulations and temptations.

19.

CHANGING PLANS AND ENCOURAGEMENTS
SEPTEMBER – OCTOBER 2014

WEDNESDAY 10TH SEPTEMBER 2014

My flight from Heathrow arrived at Entebbe Airport on time. Christine Birt and Sam Waniaye met me at Entebbe. We spent the night at the Namirembe Resource Centre in Kampala, and travelled to Mbale today.

On the way to Mbale I realised that I had left my jacket in the room at the resource centre, and my comb and diary are in the jacket. The comb and jacket are replaceable, but the information in my diary isn't. There are appointments in my diary right up to the end of next year! I intend to phone the resource centre tomorrow. I'm sure the people there must know who used the room and will be keeping them. I hope so!

FRIDAY 12TH SEPTEMBER 2014

A lady at the Namirembe Resource Centre assured me that my jacket, complete with comb and diary, were waiting for me in the office there. I'm to collect them on the way home. What a relief!

When I went to have the handouts printed the man at

the copy shop remembered me from my earlier visit this year and knew exactly what I wanted. The young lady at the coffee shop next door also remembered me and knew what I wanted. It's like I've never been away as regards to those two places.

SATURDAY 20TH SEPTEMBER 2014

Today I travelled with Osika Wilbert and Pastor Margaret to Margaret's church at Bukimuga, Bukonde District, to present the Equip Leadership training. The teaching itself was well received with seventeen (I think) participants taking handouts away with them. Bukimuga village is very beautiful, with waterfalls cascading through lush forests. It is on the side of Mount Wanale, and the road to and from the village is exceedingly dangerous, with a drop on one side! Because of the condition of the road Osika says he will change the programme for my next visit, asking those who are serious about the teaching to make their way to a lower venue, and including leaders from other churches. I'm pleased about that, as I would like to include more leaders from other churches in the programme. It's a pity about the road.

At Bukimuga I was given chicken and rice to eat. When I arrived back at Christine Birt's home she had lunch for me – chicken and rice!

MONDAY 22ND SEPTEMBER 2014

A change of plan yesterday took me to Kaleco village, Pallisa District, where I preached at a church around two years old. The people were very enthusiastic with their praises and were serious about their walk with God. We had an enjoyable time. Osika Wilbert told me that he'd been taking the Leadership teaching there, which encouraged me.

It was a long journey from Mbale to Kaleco, and as we arrived, I quipped, "Are we still in Uganda?" I told Osika and the driver, Emma (a man!), that I expected to get out of the car and find everybody speaking Portuguese! I was assured that we hadn't reached Mozambique!

The roads around Mbale are in chaos as most of the main roads, if not all of them, are being 'improved' at the same time. The planners don't appear to have made any provision for heavy vehicles. There are large lorries, nose to tail, battling through the local cars, taxis, motorcycles and push bikes. Some of the lorries have got Kenyan, Congolese and Sudanese licence plates. They are a long way from home!

Four terrorists, complete with explosives, were arrested in a guest house a short distance from Christine's home a few days ago. For a while there was a heavy police presence, but they were less apparent this morning when I walked into town.

WEDNESDAY 24TH SEPTEMBER 2014

On Monday evening Christine took me to Faith Radio where I was given the privilege of testifying to her listeners of the healing I had received under Dave Duell's ministry. This is the healing I received in 1990, when I joined Youth with a Mission, the healing I mentioned in Chapter 1.

Today, when I start to wonder if God is doing anything in my life; when I cannot see what He is doing, this miracle comes into my mind, and I am reminded that, yes, God is working in my life, even if I cannot see how.

Tuesday morning, and Christine took me to Mbale Main Prison where I preached to the church that meets there. We were at the prison on the previous Tuesday too. It was a real joy to see prisoners praising God and finding freedom in the Spirit.

SATURDAY 27TH SEPTEMBER 2014

This morning Osika Wilbert, Tom, Emma (our driver) and I abandoned our journey to Luseke, near Sironko, as both roads into the village were impassable due to heavy rain turning sections of the red-earth track into mud. We returned to the nearby town of Sironko and held a mini-conference. We decided that Osika would return to the village at a later date using a motorcycle, and present the teaching himself. For my next visit to Uganda, due in March and April next year, we plan to present the teaching at a venue in Sironko, asking the leaders to come in from Luseke and inviting more leaders from the Sironko area. Romans chapter 8, verse 28 says, 'We know that all things work together for the good of those who love God: those who are called according to His purpose'. Although not reaching the village was a setback at the time, it did allow the project to expand.

MONDAY 29TH SEPTEMBER 2014

Yesterday Osika Wilbert, Emma and I returned to Kaleco, Pallisa District, where I preached. Although the roads were passable, extreme care had to be taken in some places. Like much of the developing world there is still a lot of work to be done regarding services, such as transport, utilities (there are still regular power cuts and water cuts, where power and water are available), and the medical services. Improvements have been made in some areas, as I've noticed in the twenty-four years I've been visiting, but in other areas we are only scratching the surface. The power of the Gospel, though, is changing lives. Let us continue to encourage our missionaries in whatever ways we can.

WEDNESDAY 1ST OCTOBER 2014

This morning I was feeling very discouraged as I walked into Mbale. The roads are in such a mess and I wondered what I was doing here. Road 'improvements' are being made but the contractors have made no provision for either traffic or pedestrians. Crossing the road is difficult, and almost impossible at junctions. Even walking along the side of the road is difficult, especially following rain when the road turns to mud.

Discouragement turned to encouragement when I returned to Christine Birt's home and found Philip Lotimong waiting for me. Philip is an eager supporter of the Equip Leadership programme and he told me of his plans for using the teaching over the next few months. Philip has ongoing plans for taking the teaching into his home region of Karamoja, and across the border into Kenya. This has encouraged me very much.

As Philip was leaving Osika Wilbert arrived. Osika is also an enthusiastic supporter of the Equip Leadership teaching, and he told me of his ongoing plans to use the teaching more locally. The visits of these two dear brothers were very encouraging.

Satan attacks, I find, when we are lined up for encouragement, a blessing or a miracle. This has happened to me time and time again. We have to learn to ride the discouragements, as it were, and wait and see what God has for us.

Yesterday, Christine Birt and I went into Mbale Main Prison, where I preached. Towards the close of the meeting four prisoners came forward to accept Jesus as their Lord and Saviour. One of the four had got out of his bed in the sick bay and walked across the prison quadrangle especially to be saved. We give God the glory for this.

SATURDAY 4TH OCTOBER 2014

This morning's Equip Leadership teaching took place at Nacanyi, Pallisa District, which was a new venue with a new group of leaders. I was told after the teaching that it had been appreciated. The church leaders, I was told, could see the value of the teaching and intended to use the handouts I'd left with them to study the teaching.

At times during this visit to Uganda I've struggled with the conditions and the heat, and I know it's a spiritual attack to try and discourage me. Uganda has been a major part of my life since 1990 and the Equip Leadership programme is being a blessing by those participating. God is anointing this project. In order to live the dream and reach the target, we must be prepared to pay the price, run the race, plough through the difficulties, with our minds set upon the crown God has for us when we meet Him face-to-face. Glory be to God!

MONDAY 6TH OCTOBER 2014

Julius Hande is one of Christine Birt's key workers, and he is also a pastor at the church I preached at on Sunday morning, Hosanna Church, Namabasa. The service was a wonderful climax for my final Sunday for this visit to Uganda. A young lady by the name of Anita interpreted into the local language and flowed along with me. It was a great encouragement as I started to wind down for this visit.

Christine Birt had told me that both her key workers, Julius Hande and Sylvia Alupo, are interested in the Equip Leadership teaching, and indeed, they have separately told me so themselves. Each has received copies of the handouts. Christine has also told me that the prisoners in Mbale Main Prison also appreciated the teaching the last time I was here, so I have made sure I'm leaving copies of the handouts for Christine to give to them.

Christine gave me the opportunity of giving a plug for the Equip Leadership teaching on her programme on Top Radio last evening. We invited any church leaders who were interested in joining the programme to contact Christine, who would put them in touch with either Philip Lotimong or Osika Wilbert, who are my key men in the Mbale area for the teaching. Interest is growing!

My final ministry for this visit will be in Mbale Main Prison tomorrow. Both the Equip Leadership teaching and the preaching ministry have been blessed and anointed by God. As I wind down I'm feeling that the visit has been good and I'm already looking forward to being here again.

WEDNESDAY 8TH OCTOBER 2014

My final ministry for this visit at Mbale Main Prison was enjoyable, with the prisoners asking me to tell my own church in the UK about them.

Christine's two key workers, Julius and Sylvia, met Christine and me as we came out of prison (Julius had borrowed a car), and the four of us went to Endiro Coffee, an American-style café in the centre of Mbale, for a farewell meal together. I had honey glazed pork ribs. Very nice!

My regular stopping place for an Americano coffee (cold milk, no sugar!) is at the Café Arabica on Republic Street. I even have a loyalty card, and indeed, I've enjoyed two free coffees this visit. When I told the waitress that I was returning to the UK she said to keep the loyalty card and continue to use it the next time I am here in March. Two more Americanos and I get another free one!

THURSDAY 9TH OCTOBER 2014

My final evening at Christine Birt's home was spent with no power, no water, and to cap it all, Christine received a text from the UK High Commission saying that somebody had died from a disease called Marburg. I understand that Marburg is as deadly as Ebola!

Today Sam Waniaye drove Christine and me to Kampala, where I was reunited with my jacket, comb, and most important of all, my diary. The traffic in Kampala was solid on this, Uganda's Independence Day.

This evening Christine, Sam and I travelled to Entebbe

Airport where I'm writing this whilst waiting for my flight to Heathrow. Again, this evening the traffic was quite heavy, with motorists operating a 'me first' attitude. It's every man for himself! Many people are killed or seriously injured on Uganda's roads. Please pray for the safety of missionaries who need to travel around.

Despite all the difficulties the ministry was good, especially the Equip Leadership training. I'm already looking forward to my next visit in March!

During my time in Uganda I received a text from Jo McCabe, one of Steve Jesney's church friends in Grimsby, saying that Steve was critically ill and had around six months to live. This was stunning news, and I found it hard to take in. There are so many memories of Steve around Mbale. Christine Birt's home, the cafés and restaurants we used, the churches we visited, and in one case, Steve had helped to build, and even the roads we travelled on. It is at times like this that we can only look to God for His strength and comfort.

After I had returned to the UK Clare Spencer and I visited Steve in a care home in the village of Tetney, Lincolnshire. Steve seemed to recognise Clare and me as people he knew, but not how he knew us. When I mentioned that a lot of people in Uganda sent their love he didn't seem to understand. Uganda seemed to have gone completely out of his mind. He answered questions with a simple 'yes' or 'no'. When we told him we'd visit again he gave a hint of a smile. I think Steve appreciated being visited, even if he wasn't sure who people were. It was quite sad to see him lying in bed, knowing what his past had been like.

The journey back to Mansfield would have been difficult if Clare had not been with me. I was so grateful for Clare's support at this difficult time, and to Clare's husband, Gavin, for allowing her to travel with me.

Steve Jesney passed away at 6.30pm on Thursday 27th November 2014. My good friends Dorcas Burnett and Annette Kimber were with me when I heard the news from Steve's son, Paul Jesney. Dorcas and Annette talked and prayed with me for a while. After Dorcas and Annette had left I phoned Clare Spencer and gave her the news. After Clare and I had spoken for a while I sent a text to Christine Birt in Uganda.

Steve's funeral took place on Monday 22nd December 2014 at Louth, Lincolnshire. It was a privilege to be asked to speak, and I said:

"It was 2007, and I was midway through a twelve-month visit to Uganda, staying in the home of missionary Christine Birt in Mbale.

"One day I heard a whisper that somebody called Steve was coming back. Then more people started saying that Steve was coming back, and there was a sense of excitement in the air. So I made some enquiries.

"Steve, I discovered, had made his first appearance in Mbale the previous year, where he had been involved in an evangelistic campaign in the village of Namabasa, on the outskirts of Mbale. A church had been planted and the structure for a church building had been put in place. Steve then returned to his home in Lincolnshire, to some place called 'Louth', which I had only vaguely heard of. And now, Steve was coming back, and people were excited! I was looking forward to meeting Steve.

"Every now and then, you meet somebody for the first time, and you know instantly that you are going to be great friends. Have you noticed that? That's what happened to me when I met Steve for the first time.

"Steve was a great encouragement to me during my visits to Mbale since that time. He used his vehicle to take me out to the villages I was working in. He assessed my preaching, and wasn't afraid to tell me when I had used an illustration that, although he understood it, he knew that the Africans didn't. He took me to see projects that other missions were involved with so that I could get a wider picture of the work in the area.

"I was in Mbale when news came through that Steve would not recover from his illness. The news was received with shock by both Africans and missionaries. Steve had made his mark, and is sadly missed. I can tell you that Steve's time in Mbale is appreciated, by Christians and non-Christians alike.

"And now Steve has gone to his reward. Enjoy it, Steve. You deserve the best."

Clare and I have visited Steve's grave since that time. More visits are planned.

20.

HOW MANY WIVES DO YOU HAVE?
MARCH – APRIL 2015

WEDNESDAY 11TH MARCH 2015

On Monday I flew from Heathrow to Entebbe where I was met by Christine Birt and Sam Waniaye, who took me to the Namirembe Resource Centre in Kampala for the night. On Tuesday we travelled to Mbale.

At Mbale, in Christine's home, I unpacked my bags and Christine was delighted with the items I had taken for her, which ranged from DVDs to a food blender, and even a packet of Bassett's liquorice allsorts!

Christine and I were due to visit Mbale Main Prison this morning, but a dog bite last night saw us in the surgery at Joy Hospice, having my wound treated. I've to visit the hospice for the next three days to have the dressing changed.

FRIDAY 13TH MARCH 2015

Much of Thursday was taken up with resting and discussing the forthcoming weekend with Sam Waniaye, who came to the house. In the evening we had House Fellowship and it was good to renew friendships with Suzanne from New Zealand, and Jerome from Holland

and his Ugandan wife Petwa. Christine's house girl Sylvia Alupo also joined us. We had a meal together and then went into Bible study. Around 9.00pm, though, I had to leave the group and go to bed as I was extremely tired.

This morning Christine and I went into Mbale Main Prison where I preached. It was good to meet up once more with those who remembered me, both prisoners and staff. Two prisoners made commitments to Christ. What a privilege to be there!

MONDAY 16TH MARCH 2015

Saturday saw me taking the Equip Leadership training to Namatala, with leaders from the church there. We were also joined by Philip and Rose Lotimong from Namabasa, making fourteen of us, including myself, if I have counted correctly.

In the afternoon I had my wound dressed at the hospital.

On Sunday I preached at Namabasa. It feels so good to be ministering once more in Uganda. The dog bite, I must admit, threatened to drive me into depression, but ministering has lifted me out of it. I'm starting to trust the dogs again, too, especially the one that bit me. It was something I had to get my head around, as I couldn't spend the next few weeks being frightened of dogs!

This morning I was back at the hospital having my wound checked and dressed. The wound is healing quite quickly, for which we give God the glory!

Also this morning I had more handouts printed. When I went on Friday for the first batch the man at the print shop remembered me, and knew what I wanted. Whilst waiting for the printing I called for an Americano at my favourite coffee shop, and the girl there remembered me. It's so good to be remembered. I consider myself a regular customer at both the print shop and the coffee shop.

WEDNESDAY 18TH MARCH 2015

In this region of Uganda, with the weather being so hot and sunny, there is a desperate shortage of water. The ground is too hard for the subsistence farmers to dig in order to plant. Rain clouds hover over Mbale, with the promise of rain, but go away without depositing! The lawn at the house is almost non-existent, and the plants intended to beautify the place are wilting. The piped water supply is cut for several hours a day and water needs to be fetched from the river. We are praying that the promise of rain will be delivered soon.

Christine Birt and I went into prison on Tuesday morning to preach, but the session had to be cut short due to a number of top people arriving from Kampala. It seems that a good number of the prisoners are due to attend High Court sessions and prep work needed to be done.

My wound continues to heal, for which we can praise God.

MONDAY 23RD MARCH 2015

On Saturday Fred Masakala and I took the Equip Leadership teaching to Luseke in Sironko District. Before

I return to the UK I shall have to speak with Sam Waniaye about restructuring the training. The way it was done the previous Saturday at Namatala was ideal. At Luseke, although a number of leaders attended, some from other churches, others turned up expecting the session to be some sort of conference or crusade.

For future visits, perhaps we can present the teaching at two centres, Namatala or Namabasa, and in Sironko itself, to invited leaders, concentrating on those who are taking the training out to other places. My feeling is that the other places, in Bukonde District and a fourth place that appears to have been added on, should be serviced by local trainers who have received the teaching under me.

If the teaching can be cut to two Saturdays, this would allow me to reduce my time in Uganda. I have been invited to take the teaching to India and would need to prepare for this. If a visit to India is a success I may need to take two visits to that country each year. Other countries are showing interest too!

When I had my wound dressed this morning I overheard missionary doctor Jan White ask somebody how many wives he had. Haven't heard that in A&E before!

WEDNESDAY 25TH MARCH 2015

On Tuesday morning Christine Birt and I went into Mbale Main Prison to minister. It feels strange to say that I look forward to going into prison, but that is exactly how I feel. Ministry here, in prison and in the churches, makes the hassle of working in such a difficult country so worthwhile.

We have been watching some of Christine's wildlife

DVDs, visiting New Guinea and South America. Now that I have passed the so-called 'retirement' age I'm realising that there is so much I haven't seen, so many countries I haven't visited. Instead of slowing down, I want to speed up!

MONDAY 30TH MARCH 2015

The ministry here in Uganda goes on. On Saturday we took the Leadership training to Pastor Margaret's church at Bukimuga, Bukonde District, and on Sunday I preached at Namatala Mustard Seed Church.

At Bukimuga again, as at Luseke the previous Saturday, some of those attending had come for a 'day out' rather than serious Leadership training. The preaching at Namatala on Sunday, though, was very enjoyable. It's good to flow in the anointing of God.

FRIDAY 3RD APRIL 2015

What a depressing day today is! Yesterday afternoon the power went off, and it is still off as I write this almost twenty-four hours later. This morning, when I went to the cash machine, hoping to withdraw an amount of money, I found the machine turned off. Being Good Friday, and therefore a public holiday, the bank was closed. The security guard, however, told me that the system was down and to come back in two hours. I decided to try again this afternoon. Afternoon has now arrived, and we have rain! I am hoping that the rain will stop soon; then I will try the cash machine again.

If I cannot access my money, I cannot pay for a vehicle to take me to Nacanyi for Equip Leadership training tomorrow, or to Kaleco to preach on Sunday. That's how things are in Uganda.

PS. Just been to the toilet and the water is off!

MONDAY 6TH APRIL 2015

Just had a very encouraging weekend. On Saturday Sam Waniaye took me to Nacanyi to present the Equip Leadership teaching. This is a village that I didn't really want to go to as I felt that one of the local leaders should have been presenting the teaching. I was so much encouraged that I realised this village needs to be included in the programme. As I have already determined that Sironko, along with Namatala and Namabasa, need to be included. This means that, in future visits, I need to be in Uganda for three Saturdays rather than just the two Saturdays I was hoping for. We need to be flexible with our plans, under God's leading.

On Sunday, Easter Day, Osika Wilbert, David Livingstone and I went to the village of Kaleco in Pallisa District, where I preached. Two women were delivered from demons and one of them received Jesus Christ as her Lord and Saviour. It was such a privilege to be there and to take part in the service.

THURSDAY 9TH APRIL 2015

Well, this is it – almost at the end of my visit. Today is the final full day. Looking back, although there have been some challenges, the visit has been generally successful. The Equip Leadership training has been especially blessed, which was the primary reason for being here.

On Wednesday Sam Waniaye, David Livingstone, Fred Masakala, Philip Lotimong and I met and discussed my next visit, planned for September. We agreed that next time the teaching will be held at three centres over three Saturdays: Namatala/Namabasa, Sironko and Nacanyi. We also discussed publishing reports from those taking the teaching out in my monthly newsletter, perhaps one each month. Also, we talked about certificates for those taking part, but we agreed to leave that for a while until it became clear who the serious people are; those who are attending each time and passing the teaching on to other churches in other villages. Another matter I mentioned is that Julius Hande, who works for Christine Birt, had asked me if I could preach at his church when I came in September, and Sam made a note of it.

All in all, it's been a very encouraging visit, and I am now looking forward to getting back to Mansfield. Although I know I'm going to be busy for the first three weeks or so, I am looking forward to seeing people back in Mansfield who I know care for me.

21.

THANK YOU FOR BANKING WITH US
SEPTEMBER 2015

FRIDAY 11ᵀᴴ SEPTEMBER 2015

Wednesday morning, and it was time for my flight for my latest visit to Uganda. The check-in and baggage drop went smoothly, but as I was passing through security, I realised that I had left my coat with my hat in the pocket draped over the back of a chair in the restaurant I had used in the terminal. Never mind. Too late to do anything about it, and both coat and hat could be replaced.

We passengers boarded the plane, and as we were just about to take off, a passenger took ill and needed to be let off the plane. This was done, and a crew of baggage handlers arrived, unloaded the bags from the plane, identified the passenger's luggage and reloaded the plane. This made take-off one hour later than scheduled. Good time was made, however, and we landed at Entebbe just half an hour late.

Christine Birt and Sam Waniaye met me at Entebbe, and after spending the night in Kampala, we travelled to Mbale, reaching our destination on Thursday afternoon.

This morning, Julius Hande and I walked into town where we had the handouts printed ready for the first session of teaching tomorrow. Whilst in town I bought myself a new hat, called at a computer shop and greeted Ben, our friendly computer man, and had coffee in my favourite coffee shop where the waitress complained that she hadn't seen me for a long time!

MONDAY 14TH SEPTEMBER 2015

The first Equip Leadership training took place on Saturday at Namatala, with participants from Namabasa and two churches in Bukonde. It was good to meet up once more with leaders such as Sam Waniaye, Philip and Rose Lotimong, David Livingstone, Rose Opio, Osika Wilbert and others. God's anointing was felt very strongly upon the teaching, and it appeared to be appreciated by all the participants.

God's anointing was evident on Sunday morning too, also at Namatala. The whole of the service – the leading, the worship, the ministry and everything else – flowed along under God's Spirit. My ministry was based on Acts chapter 2, The Fulfilment of the Prophecy of Joel, with the emphasis being on the way God used Peter in spite of Peter messing up. God can use us no matter what our situation is.

The power of the Holy Spirit changes people. In verse 14 onwards Peter stood up to preach. Peter was the one who denied Jesus. In Luke chapter 22, verse 33 Peter had told Jesus, "I'm ready to go with You both to prison and to death!" Then in verses 54 to 62 we find Peter denying Jesus. Then here, in Acts chapter 2, the Spirit comes and we find Peter full of boldness, proclaiming Jesus as Lord and Messiah.

Quite often we know that we were just like Peter. We messed up and did some things we wished we'd never done. But God took us and gave us another chance. Perhaps some of us are living in the messed-up position now, or at least we think we are. We are very good at beating ourselves up over issues that have already been dealt with. I've got news for you. God is able to pick us up, shake the mess off us, and use us in His service. We can live in the power of His Holy Spirit, and all the glory goes to Him.

THURSDAY 17TH SEPTEMBER 2015

On Tuesday, fellowship was renewed with the residents of Mbale Main Prison when I made a visit with Christine Birt. Quite a few of the men in the church that meets there remembered me from my visit to Uganda earlier this year. My message was taken from Acts chapter 4, when Peter and John were brought before the court to explain their actions after the healing of the lame man.

We need to look at the background to this story to understand the situation the Sadducees were in. In chapter 3 Peter and John were going up together to the Temple when they came across a man who had been lame all his life. He was begging, and he asked Peter and John for help.

Peter looked at the man and said, "Look at us." The man looked at them, expecting to get something from them. Peter said to the man, "I have neither silver nor gold, but what I have, I give to you: in the Name of Jesus Christ the Nazarene, get up and walk!" Peter took the man's right hand, raised him up, and his feet and ankles became strong. The man jumped up, stood, and then started to walk. He entered the Temple with Peter and John, walking, leaping and praising God.

Jeff Lucas, writing on this passage in Lucas on Life (CWR), says, It's rather inconvenient when our carefully crafted beliefs prove to be false. The Sadducees, who didn't believe in the resurrection of the dead, were now in the most terrible jam, because a man who had suffered from lifelong disabilities was standing among them, healed in the name of the risen Jesus. Responding with stubbornness rather than faith, they threatened Peter and John, who made the simple retort – we have to speak about what we know. There's no negotiation. The fear that had caused Peter to deny was gone now. So what has changed?

Jeff Lucas then goes on to talk about how the disciples had changed through the power of the Holy Spirit on the Day of Pentecost. We sometimes find ourselves in situations where we have to speak. We cannot remain silent. Quite often, I find myself in situations where I ought to speak, but I stay silent. But sometimes we have to speak. A power comes over us, and we find ourselves with a strength, and wisdom, which we know doesn't belong to us. We say what we feel we must say, and then we think to ourselves, Where did that come from? The power of the Holy Spirit gives us the courage to do things we wouldn't normally do.

Wednesday evening saw the Missionary Fellowship at Christine's home. It was good to share fellowship once more with Jerome and Petwa who operate Dutch Farm, a dairy farm producing milk, cheese (including Gouda), and yoghurt. I had seen Jerome earlier in the day whilst in Mbale, driving his motor-tricycle pickup. I stood on the central reservation of the dual carriageway of Kumi Road, just to see how observant he was – and he stopped. But then, I'm the one who misses people. Only this morning I was walking by a parked car when a voice said, "David Ardron." When I turned around I saw Andrew Mutenga, who was sitting in the car. I have known Andrew since the Kamuli days!

SUNDAY 20ᵀᴴ SEPTEMBER 2015

On Thursday we received visitors from the UK: Roy and Rosemary Saunders, and Stuart and Rebeccah Scott, who all live in Forest Town, Mansfield. Roy and Rosemary were visiting Uganda for the first time, Stuart has made a number of visits, and Stuart's wife, Rebeccah, is Ugandan. Rosemary ministered on Christine's radio programme on Thursday evening.

Roy and Rosemary visited again on Friday, and in the evening, Christine and I went to the Sunrise Hotel to meet with Alwyn and Mary Griffiths, from Merthyr Tydfil, who were visiting a school that their charity, Ezra, had built and was now running at Bunabutye, beyond Sironko. Roy, Rosemary, Stuart and Rebeccah were staying at the same hotel, and the eight of us pushed three tables together in the dining room and shared fellowship over a meal.

On Saturday, Sam Waniaye and Osika Wilbert collected me with a Land Cruiser, and after calling at the Sunrise Hotel for Roy Saunders, we travelled to Sironko for a presentation of the Equip Leadership training. Around twenty people attended, mostly pastors from the surrounding village churches, who promised to pass on the teaching to their own leaders. It was so encouraging. The whole visit is encouraging this time as I can see the work taking root and blossoming.

This morning Julius Hande collected me and took me to Namabasa where I preached on Ephesians chapter 6, The Whole Armour of God. After the close of the service, as I waited for Julius, who had gone to his own church which is close by, I saw a distribution of shoeboxes containing gifts for the children which had been received from Operation Christmas Child. If you contribute towards this project, or help in any way, I can tell you that your gifts and efforts are very much appreciated.

WEDNESDAY 23RD SEPTEMBER 2015

As I write this I am sat on the veranda of Christine's home, chilling out after eating lunch. In front of me there is a lawn. The lawn is patchy due to the constant animal traffic: cows, donkeys, eight dogs (some of which are cavorting about on the lawn as I write), two cats, and the use of the lawn as a car park. Around the boundary of the property a chain link fence is covered in foliage, giving privacy, and a number of trees are immediately in front of the veranda, giving even more privacy. The species of the trees, and various other plants and flowers, will have to remain a mystery. As far as nature is concerned I can tell the difference between a daffodil and a dandelion, and that is about my limit.

Going further afield, Julius Hande introduced me to a new route into town, avoiding the roadworks that are still prevalent in Mbale, especially on Pallisa Road.

Turning right out of the gate of Christine's home, we walked downhill along a potholed road and across a fairly smooth, fairly wide, and very dusty road, onto a path that passes the back entrance of Joy Hospice, two schools, a Presbyterian church and onto Kumi Road.

Turning right onto Kumi Road we walked along a new pavement at the side of a new road; part of the legacy of the completed part of the roadworks. The pavement is smooth and a joy to walk on, apart from the drainage culverts of around six inches wide, which could trip an unwary pedestrian. On this stretch of the walk I saw a grey squirrel, which excited me until I remembered I could see grey squirrels in Sherwood Forest, a few miles from where I live in the UK. It might have been a different species. I hope so, although I wouldn't have known the difference.

We continued along an uphill slope, with me telling myself it was downhill on the way back, until the road became a dual carriageway, where we crossed the road. It was at this point I had met Jerome, mentioned previously. After a couple of turnings along nondescript roads (nondescript only because I lack imagination) we appeared on Republic Street close to my favourite coffee shop, where I threw the waiter off balance as, during the time I had been back in the UK, I'd changed my preference from Americano to latte.

There are a number of ATMs in town but we have to be careful where we stick our British debit cards. The options are down to two, with a third option to be used as a last resort as this machine charges a fee large enough to make us shout, "What?!" at the top of our voice, startling any person, animal or bird within a radius of fifty yards.

My favourite machine is the one that says, "Thank you for banking with us" when we withdraw cash. My reply is, "Thank you for giving me some money."

I wish my descriptions could be better. I don't mention the weather much. Unless I mention otherwise, such as a violent thunderstorm blowing the lights out and making us fearful of the glass coming out of the windows, then this is Africa, so assume it is hot and sunny!

FRIDAY 25TH SEPTEMBER 2015

On Tuesday morning Rosemary Saunders ministered in Mbale Main Prison with Christine, and Christine took me into the prison on Thursday morning instead of Tuesday. Thursday was a Muslim festival, and because it was a public holiday, we were not sure if we'd be allowed to enter. Fellowship was sweet, as usual, and I preached on the Whole Armour of God (Ephesians chapter 6). One sticky point was when I attempted to describe the game of chess. Twenty-five years of visiting Uganda and I'm still getting myself tied up in knots over illustrations.

After prison Christine and I took Julius and Sylvia to the Mount Elgon Hotel where we all enjoyed pork chops Hawaiian with honey mustard sauce. Beautiful! Sylvia and Julius told us that, although they have lived in the Mbale area all their lives, it was only the second time they had visited this hotel, and the first time had also been with Christine and me, during my previous visit earlier this year.

On Saturday 26th September we had the final session of Equip Leadership teaching at Nacanyi, Pallisa District.

Again the teaching was appreciated, with those taking part promising to pass the teaching on to others.

The following day I preached at Hosanna Church, Namabasa, where Julius is part of the leadership team. A young lady with a Muslim background made a decision for Jesus and I had the privilege of praying for her. It was such a blessing.

On the Sunday afternoon I met with the team who had coordinated my visit, Sam Waniaye, Philip Lotimong, David Livingstone and Osika Wilbert, to discuss how the visit had gone, and the way forward. The visit has been very encouraging. I am delighted at the way the teaching is being received and used. The team said that they would organise follow-up to ensure the teaching was passed on to others. I appreciate that.

The following day, Monday, I started my journey back to Mansfield, with Christine Birt and Sam Waniaye driving me to Entebbe Airport. The journey homewards went smoothly and I arrived in Mansfield on Tuesday teatime.

On Tuesday 20th October 2015, until Friday 23rd, I attended an Equip Leadership event at Pebble Beach, California. It was a ten-hour flight from Heathrow to San Francisco, and I passed the time by following the progress on the moving map. It was fascinating to watch the map as we flew over Ireland, then over Iceland and Greenland. We continued over the short stretch of water to northeast Canada, over the northern edge of Hudson Bay, then on to Edmonton and Calgary, and over the Rocky Mountains to San Francisco. We flew over all these places. Never saw them – just flew over them!

Whilst on the plane my mind was plagued with doubts, such as, *What are you doing, David? You're flying to a country you've never been to before, and you don't know anybody there. What on earth are you doing?*

These were the thoughts in my mind as we landed at San Francisco. After passing through Immigration and Baggage Reclaim without any problem I was met by Nicholas Kromer of Main Event Transportation, who very ably drove me in a Mercedes Benz sedan for the two-hour journey from San Francisco Airport to The Inn at Spanish Bay, Pebble Beach.

My thoughts were still negative as we arrived at the hotel. Because of the lateness of my arrival one of the reception staff took my bags to my room, and I went into the first meeting just as I had arrived, with no chance of tidying myself up!

The participants were gathered in the hallway before joining the meeting, and some of them chatted with me. Those who did were very interested when they discovered I had made the journey from the UK, and that I was using the Equip Leadership curriculum in Uganda. I was introduced to Tom Mullins, the Chairman of Equip, and Charlie Wetzel remembered me from Stoke-on-Trent. Charlie was one of the two men, along with Mark Middleton, who led the training days at Stoke-on-Trent. We collected our buffet meals and I found a place at a table. The folks already sat at the table welcomed me and made me feel at ease.

When we had finished our meals, and the meeting started, I realised why I was there; why I had made the effort. It was very encouraging and uplifting to hear reports of how God is using the Equip Leadership teaching in other parts of the world. The real confirmation, though, came when John Maxwell gave a short talk. These days I'm an avid reader of John Maxwell's books, but hearing him speak a very encouraging message made me realise that I had made the correct decision in making the long journey to be there.

On the morning of Wednesday 21st, the encouragement continued. After I had collected my breakfast I sat a table with Tom Mullins and others, who made me feel very welcome. Again, being from the UK (I think I was the only person there who wasn't American!), and using the teaching in Uganda, opened the door for conversations. It was a real encouragement to be mixing with people who were using the Equip programme in various ways.

In the daytime there was a golf tournament in progress, which, being a non-golfer, I took no part in. Instead, I treated the time as a retreat. After breakfast I took a walk along a path that led to a beach where I sat on a bench, looking out over the Pacific Ocean, which I was seeing for the first time. Behind me, the golfers were excitedly putting their stuff.

In the afternoon, I sat on the back lawn of the hotel and brought my journal up to date. Whilst I was relaxing, letting my mind wander, two harts wandered out of the forest just beyond the lawn, and nibbled on the grass. The sun was quite warm, perhaps around 28 degrees Celsius, and it was rather pleasant to be sat there. I placed my pen and notebook on the table in front of me and simply soaked in the sun.

I wish very much that I could remember the names of

the people I speak with! On the Wednesday evening I got into a conversation with a man who had a connection with the new Salt and Light programme that John Maxwell has been working on. The man asked if he could help in any way with my work using the Equip Leadership programme in Uganda. I told him that we wanted to have the teaching materials translated into Luganda, the Ugandan national language. The man (I wish I could remember his name!) told me that the new Salt and Light initiative included Equip Leadership material, and that translators were needed for other languages. People who could be trusted were being sought in the countries concerned. The man took my business card and there may be an opportunity to be involved in this exciting new project. We will see.

In the meeting various speakers who were involved with the new initiative, including John Maxwell himself, spoke about the Salt and Light project and it all sounded very exciting. The following morning I got around to reading some of the booklets I'd been handed on arrival and found that Salt and Light had been fully explained in one of them, and it sounded even more exciting.

Thursday morning came, and I took a walk on the beach for the last time for this visit. Whilst I was sitting on a bench, watching the waves and the surfers, some of whom actually stayed on their boards, I saw two women who looked as though they belonged in a Brontë story. After a while I realised that they must have been Amish. God bless the Amish!

Looking back at the visit, although I was apprehensive on my journey there, I was greatly blessed when I arrived. This happens so often, at least it does to me, when we are apprehensive about going to a place and we struggle to make an effort. We arrive, and receive a blessing.

Am I going next year? The date is already in my diary!

Since the happenings above, two of the leaders in Mbale, Sam Waniaye and Osika Wilbert, have discovered an agency in Uganda who have very capably translated some of the teaching into Luganda. Sam has examined the work and says that the translation is accurate and that the ethos hasn't been lost. (Somebody once returned from a visit to Rome and told me that they'd seen 'Warm Dogs' for sale in a café!)

We thank God for His supply.

APPENDIX

IS GOD CALLING YOU?

WHAT GETS YOU OUT OF BED IN THE MORNING?

What gets you out of bed in the morning? For some of us it might be the overwhelming desire to visit the bathroom very quickly. The question I am asking here is what makes us want to get out of bed, get dressed and launch ourselves into the day?

We could drift through life without the desire to do anything at all. Michael Holliday sang a song about having nothin' to do and nowhere to go. This would send me up the wall!

But what gets us out of bed when we have retired from paid work? Note that I use the phrase 'retired from paid work' rather than simply using the word 'retired'. There is a difference. If we are Christians, followers of Jesus Christ, then I believe that we never retire from His service. Have you ever wondered why God didn't take us to be with Him when we made a decision to accept the salvation offered to us through His Son, Jesus Christ? It's because, I believe, God has work for us to do. As long as we are here on earth there is something God wants us to do, and He will not take us until our task here is complete.

So, we have come to the end of our paid work. We are coming up to our sixty-fifth birthday and we are due to receive our state pension. Or we are in our fifties and we have been paying into a private pension. We've reached the position where we can 'retire', take a lump sum and receive a monthly income from our pension provider. Or we may suffer a serious illness which comes out of the blue.

In November 2000, at the age of fifty-two, I suffered a serious heart attack which left me with three quarters heart damage. In October 2001 I underwent triple bypass heart surgery to improve the blood flow to the part of my heart that was still working properly. In June 2005, after recuperating, I returned to work, albeit with a different company, part-time and in a lower-paid job with fewer responsibilities. After eighteen months I took the opportunity to 'retire early'.

Many younger people have a gap year when they take a year out from university, or between university and starting work, to carry out voluntary work, either in this country or overseas, or to simply travel and open themselves up to new experiences. At the age of fifty-eight, I took the gap year that I never had in my younger days.

In 1990 I had taken a Discipleship Training School with Youth with a Mission. Included in the school was five weeks' outreach in Kenya and Uganda. Since that time I have returned to Uganda many times for visits of various lengths between two weeks and four months. For my gap year I took the opportunity of visiting Uganda for twelve months, to preach in village churches.

When I returned to Mansfield in January 2008 I came back to an empty life. As I had been away for twelve months there was no ministry for me. No preaching appointments or anything else. A friend had found a small flat for me, which was so ideal that I stayed there for six years. However, it was in an unfamiliar part of town. In the town familiar buildings had been demolished, and new buildings had been erected. Although some areas of Mansfield looked the same, other areas could have been a different town. Although the church building was the same, some members had died or moved away and new members had joined.

My time away from Mansfield had been only twelve months. If you have missionaries from your fellowship working overseas, please don't assume that they can return and simply drop into the local scene. Hometowns, sometimes places where they have grown up, look different. Shops change, buildings are in different places, and I've heard of missionaries letting buses go by at bus stops as they hadn't realised a different company had taken over the route. The people in the church are different. One missionary I know returned to her hometown only to discover that her sending church had closed. Everybody had assumed that somebody else had told her.

In her book Honourably Wounded (Monarch, 2001) Marjory F. Foyle gives an excellent description of the feelings of returning missionaries, both from her own experience and from professional research. Dr Foyle's book was written several years ago, but it gives us some idea of the kind of things returning missionaries, and other ex-pats for that matter, face. Every year there is something new to catch people out!

When local church secretaries realised I was back in Mansfield the bookings for preaching started to arrive, and my preaching ministry was soon back on track. Before leaving for my gap year in Uganda I had mentioned to the minister of my church that I had seen a course entitled An Introduction to Spiritual Direction, advertised by CWR. My minister suggested that I take the course, which I did. This led to a further course on the same subject, offered by the Diocese of Southwell and Nottingham, which in turn led to a fulfilling ministry.

If we are willing, and if we are open to His calling, God always has more for us to do. I would encourage you to move forward, under God's guidance, into the wonderful future He has for you. The world is wide open for those who are willing to step out in obedience, and grasp the opportunities that are open for His people.

When we know that God is leading us, we are motivated. When we are motivated, excitement swells up inside of us. We want to get on with whatever task God has allotted to us. We resent other things getting in the way, and this could be a danger. Whilst writing this appendix I still had sermons to prepare, I still had a monthly report to send out to prayer supporters, and I had teaching on Leadership to prepare for Uganda. There were also other duties for church to tend to, and of course, people in my life to spend time with.

But there are things that get in the way that we can push out of our lives in order to get on with the work God has given us. We can watch less television, we can listen to less radio, we can read fewer novels, and we can be wary of computer games. My time-waster is computer solitaire. I find it addictive, and once I have started playing, I cannot stop until I have completed the game. It can take as long as five hours! Then I go into a depression because I have wasted time when I could have been getting on with something more productive. What is your time-waster?

The flip side of motivation is restoration. Do today's younger people know what a flip side is? When we bought our music on 45rpm vinyl discs the flip side was the side of the record that the jocks on the radio never played. And the flip side of motivation is restoration.

It is important for us to step aside and refresh our bodies, our minds and our spirits. We need to take regular breaks. Sunday, of course, is the day for church, but we need to take other days or part-days off too. We need to make sure we have hobbies or pastimes. You may notice above that I have written that we can watch less television or read fewer novels – my intention is not that we cut them out altogether. A good walk always refreshes my mind. And of course, if we have a spouse or other family members we must not neglect them. We need to find the balance.

The writer of Hebrews chapter 4, verses 10 to 11a sums it up nicely: "For the person who has entered His rest has rested from his own works, just as God did from His. Let us then make every effort to enter that rest…"

WHY DO WE WORK?

Why do we work? Why don't we simply exist, get out of bed in the morning (who constructed the bed?), sit in our house (who built the house?), watching television (who made the set and the programme we are watching?), and then go back to bed? God created us for a purpose, and we need to find that purpose.

We could be working for financial reasons – we work in order to live. We could be career-chasing; we need to be the best we can be and reach the top of the tree – we live in order to work. Or we may have the desire to improve the lives of others – we live and work to make a difference. The latter is the difference between a job and a vocation.

The world came into existence through God working. Genesis chapter 1, verse 1 says, "In the beginning God created the heavens and the earth". God worked to create the world for us to live in. God also expects us to work. Genesis chapter 1, verse 26 says, Then God said, "Let Us make man in Our image, according to Our likeness. They will rule the fish of the sea, the birds of the sky, the animals, all the earth, and the creatures that crawl on the earth."

What are the implications of being made in God's image? Being made in God's image doesn't mean we look like Him. We have the potential of reflecting God's character, and a part of His character is to be active. In Genesis chapter 1, verse 26 God gave us the authority to rule over the earth, and all the creatures on earth. This is a major responsibility!

Ephesians chapter 2, verse 10 sums it up nicely: "For we are His creation – created in Christ Jesus for good works, which God prepared ahead of time so that we should walk in them." We work to fulfil emotional needs. We know that we have a purpose, and the need is deep inside us. The need is designed to be met in Christ Jesus.

DON'T BE AFRAID OF CHANGE

Change is happening all the time. Some changes we hardly notice. Somebody might leave our place of work and be replaced by somebody else. If this happens in another department it might not affect us too much, and we carry on much as before. But if the person who shares our office changes then we need to get used to a new personality. We cannot expect a new colleague to be exactly like the one they have replaced, and we have to get used to their style of working.

When ill health made me drop out of work in 2000 I was proficient with a certain accounting computer package called Sage Line 50. When I returned to work in 2005, and found that my new company was using Sage Line 50, I thought I was going to be in my element. However, the package had changed so much it was like I'd never seen Sage Line 50 before! If I had carried on working during those missing years, I would have hardly noticed the changes as they would have come little by little. By going back to Sage Line 50 after a number of years, what should have been a series of small changes had turned into a major change.

In a lifetime of work we see many changes. Do you remember slide rules? In one job I used a slide rule. Slide rules have now been replaced by calculators, and we even have computer programs, such as Sage Line 50 mentioned above, that make calculations as we enter figures into boxes. When our office manager, back in the 80s, told us that computers were coming into the office, and that we had to learn how to use them, he almost found himself with an empty office! But we persevered, and we now have computers in our homes as well as in our places of work.

As I write this the generation I am a member of have mostly retired from paid work, and the generation below us is in the process of retiring. Who knows what the generation behind us is bringing into retirement? Those of us who have retired into voluntary work need to be open to the generations retiring after us bringing ideas with them that sound like science fiction. When I was a child, if my parents wanted to use a telephone, they had to walk a mile to the next village to use the public phone outside the post office. Later we had phones in our houses, and now we have phones in our pockets! The only mobile phones I saw in my younger years were in a science fiction television series – "Beam me up, Scotty!"

When we leave paid work, and move into voluntary work, we will probably find a change in our finances. The best time to start preparing for a change in our finances is whilst we are still in paid work, especially if we are in debt. Of course, it would be better not to be in debt in the first place, but we need to start from where we are, not from where we ought to be! Have you noticed how, when people try to help us with our problems, they are very good at telling us what we should have done? This isn't helpful one little bit. We cannot rewind our lives in the way we rewind a videotape (do you remember videotapes?). The future is in front, not behind.

If you are in debt, whether it be credit cards, loans,

payment plans or whatever, then get out of debt, and stay out of debt. If the task is too onerous for you then you need to take advice. Organisations exist that can help you with this, and Christians Against Poverty (CAP) were of tremendous help to me in this matter.

Bob Gass, writing in the daily Bible-reading notes Word for Today (UCB, 25th January 2013), quotes American radio show host Clark Howard, who starts every programme by saying, "Spend less, save more, and don't get ripped off." In the same notes Bob Gass says, "'But I'm used to a certain lifestyle,' you say. Get unused to it! If you want peace of mind, learn the art of contentment. Does contentment mean you can't have ambition? No, it means delaying gratification and enjoying where you are, on your way to where you're going.'

Bob Gass suggests that we learn to live by the words of the apostle Paul, who said, in Philippians chapter 4, verses 11 and 12, "I have learned to be content in whatever circumstances I am. I know both how to have a little, and I know how to have a lot. In any and all circumstances I have learned the secret [of being content] – whether well-fed or hungry, whether in abundance or in need."

LETTING GOD GUIDE

Maybe we have the desire to use the skills and experience we have gained in the voluntary sector, and we are considering joining an organisation working overseas. We need to look at the practical issues. Is there a partner to consider? If you are reading this book, you are probably a Christian. Does your partner share your faith? Many people become Christians after they have married, and their partners never follow them into the faith. If your partner is a Christian, do they share your calling? A young couple I know responded separately at a mission meeting when the speaker asked those feeling called to the mission field to stand. They went on to a fulfilling ministry in Nepal.

If your partner is not a Christian, or does not share what you feel is your calling, then it's a good indication that God might be calling you to work locally, perhaps with your local church, or an organisation working in your area. Mission does not necessarily mean going overseas. We cannot tell an unsaved partner that God is calling us to plant a church in a jungle village. For a start, it's probably untrue as God knows your situation and is quite capable of working within any limitations in your life. Of course, you could pray for your partner's salvation, but you should be doing that anyway.

We can look at the life of Jesus and see the purpose God had for His life. John chapter 1, verse 14, says, "The

Word became flesh and took up residence among us. We observed His glory, the glory as the One and Only Son from the Father, full of grace and truth."

Jesus knew what His calling and purpose was. Luke chapter 4, verses 18 and 19, says, 'The Spirit of the Lord is on Me, because He has anointed Me to preach good news to the poor. He has sent Me to proclaim freedom to the captives and recovery of sight to the blind, to set free the oppressed, to proclaim the year of the Lord's favour.'

Jesus fulfilled His purpose because He lived on purpose. He knew what His mission was and He stuck with it. Jesus had to make choices. He chose to spend time with God. He chose to use His gifts in many different ways. He chose to build relationships. We should not go far wrong if we make the same choices.

God has a purpose for our life and we need to seek to fulfil it. 2 Peter chapter 1, verse 3, tells us that we have everything we need. For His divine power has given us everything required for life and godliness, through the knowledge of Him who called us by His own glory and goodness. Let us live our lives on purpose!

We can make choices. John C. Maxwell, quoted in the seminar notes for Career Choices and Changes, presented by Stephen and Rosalyn Derges at CWR's Waverley Abbey House on 28th September 2012, says, "Everything you now do is something you have chosen to do. Some people don't want to believe that. But if you're over age twenty-one, your life is what you're making of it. To change your life, you need to change your priorities."

We find God's purpose for our lives by choosing to

spend time with Him, by choosing to discover our gifts and choosing to use them. Also, we need to follow the example of Jesus and build relationships. We need people around us!

We need to know what our potential is. We can too often put ourselves down, thinking that we are too insignificant. We need to know what God thinks about us. Psalm 139 is a wonderful, beautiful description of God's goodness in our lives. Read the entire Psalm and let the word of God refresh you as you close your eyes and meditate on these encouraging words.

David wrote, in Psalm 139, verse 14, 'I will praise You, because I have been remarkably and wonderfully made. Your works are wonderful, and I know this very well.'

David did not have the information we have today regarding our bodies when he wrote the psalm. Perhaps he was out in the fields watching the sheep and noticed how his hands had been formed. David spent time considering how remarkably and wonderfully his body had been formed.

David also wrote, in verse 15, 'My bones were not hidden from You when I was made in secret, when I was formed in the depths of the earth.'

Where my Bible, the Holman, uses 'formed', the New International Version says 'woven together'. David was so impressed with the wonder of God's gift of life that he spoke of it as being 'woven together', and here he was using the example of a craftsman who skilfully weaves a beautiful and colourful tapestry. What David was basically saying was, "I didn't just happen. I am not an accident. I have value. I have worth."

David arrived at this conclusion because he first focused on God. He realised that he was a valuable individual because he recognised he had been created by God. It was God who gave his life value. It was God who gave him worth. David recognised that, without God, his life had no value.

Our value doesn't depend upon our strengths. Our value depends upon God. Our worth to ourselves is increased as we realise how much we mean to God.

God says that when He wants something done it's going to be done (Zechariah chapter 4, verse 6), '"Not by strength or by might, but by My Spirit," says the LORD of Hosts.'

Throughout Scripture, when God wanted something done, according to Paul in 1 Corinthians chapter 1, verses 27 to 29, 'He has chosen the world's foolish things to shame the wise, and God has chosen the world's weak things to shame the strong. God has chosen the world's insignificant and despised things – the things viewed as nothing – so He might bring to nothing the things that are viewed as something, so that no one can boast in His presence.'

In Psalm 139, verses 1 to 6, David wrote, 'LORD, You have searched me and known me, You know when I sit down and when I stand up; You understand my thoughts from far away. You observe my travels and my rest; You are aware of all my ways. Before a word is on my tongue, You know all about it, LORD. You have encircled me; You have placed Your hand on me. [This] extraordinary knowledge is beyond me. It is lofty; I am unable to [reach] it.'

This could be a frightening psalm if we are not right with God. God sees everything there is to see about us, even what we are thinking. And it's not just that God sees everything; He knows everything there is to know. We cannot hide anything from God.

Verse 1 says that God has searched us, that is, He has explored us. There is a program on our computers that will carry out a scan, searching for viruses and other faults. When we ask God to search us, we are asking Him to scan us, to explore our bodies, searching for anything that needs putting right.

Some years ago I had an angiogram. A surgeon put a narrow tube through my groin, into a vein, and from there onwards and into my heart. Then he pumped some sort of liquid through the tube. Any medical people will have to forgive my description, as I wasn't really watching what he was doing! The liquid went through in spasms. The idea was, I think, that readings came onto a screen to show what condition my heart was in. Each time there was a spasm it made me jerk a little, and an attractive nurse stroked my cheek. I would have enjoyed having my cheek stroked had the circumstances been different!

When God searches us He gives us a spiritual angiogram. He digs into our life; he looks intently.

The second part of verse 2 says that God understands our thoughts from far away. God can get inside of our heads. He can see what's going on in there. Doctors can do amazing things with body scans and all the other technology that's available today, but God can see everything inside. God can see our thoughts as well as our physical bodies. God knows everything we've ever thought about. That could be quite frightening if our relationship with Him isn't right.

Verse 4 tells us that God knows the words we are going to say before we even speak them. Have you ever said something, and then wished you hadn't? I'm well known for being a slow eater, and one time I was on a dinner date with a lady. She had finished her meal well before me, and she passed a remark about me being slow. I just managed to stop myself from saying that I thought my stomach might be smaller than hers. Can you imagine?

God is aware of everything about us, everything we do and everything we think. He knows what we do in private as well as what we do in public. He knows more about us than we want Him to know.

David says, in verse 6, that this extraordinary knowledge is beyond him. It blows him away just thinking about it. When we realise that God knows us, scrutinises us and studies us twenty-four hours a day, seven days a week, it blows our mind trying to comprehend it.

These should be sobering thoughts for those who are not living in a right relationship with God. When we stand before God on the Day of Judgement there are going to be no secrets. There's going to be no hope that God didn't pay much attention to what our life was all about. He knows everything.

If we are a faithful child of God then the thought of Him knowing all about us is comforting, and the comfort comes at the very end of the psalm. In verses 23 and 24 David says, Search me, God, and know my heart; test me and know my concerns. See if there is any offensive way in me; lead me in the everlasting way.

David is asking God to search him even more intensely. He wants God to penetrate his outer shell and dig down deeply within him.

Search me and know my heart could only be spoken by someone who feels completely loved and accepted. God sees every little bit of our lives and He still loves us. He never withholds His love, even though we are prone to straying away from the path He has set us on.

We have established that God knows us, and loves us. The important question now is – do we know God? Do we know God as a loving Father who sees our faults and loves us unconditionally? This is the relationship God desires to have with us. Do we have the same desire?

We need to know what our life purpose is. As we head into another phase of our lives it is good to look at our lives and consider what our calling is; the work that God is calling us to carry out in His name. Many organisations, churches and businesses have a mission statement which describes the activities they carry out.

Selwyn Hughes wrote about creating a mission statement in his book *Spoken from the Heart, Volume 2* (CWR, 2006), giving his own mission statement as an example. After I read the book I felt impressed to write down my own personal mission statement, as Dr Hughes suggested. Here is my personal mission statement: To encourage people to deepen their relationships with God, and to fulfil His calling on their lives.

Have you got a personal mission statement? What is God's calling on your life? What is the overwhelming desire in your heart? As the opening words of this appendix asks, what gets you out of bed in the morning? As we move forward with our lives, let us consider where God is leading us, and may His purpose in our lives be fulfilled.

Another quote from the seminar Career Choices and Changes, mentioned earlier in this appendix. This time the quote is from Mark Twain, who says, 'The secret of getting ahead is getting started. The secret of getting started is breaking your complex, overwhelming tasks into small manageable tasks, then starting on the first one.'

Some time ago I heard a writer, who specialised in historical biography, being interviewed on the radio. The writer said that he found the hardest part of writing a book was to actually start on it. He said that he could research and research and research, but to actually start writing the book was quite difficult. Once he had made a start, he sailed along.

Both Mark Twain and the writer above are right. We need to make a start. We can retire with good intentions of doing all sorts of things, but we will start next week, then the week after, and so on. Then one day our ambitions have gone. We have got used to drifting along, and all we have to look forward to is regret.

We do need to research, but we also need a limit to our research, otherwise research becomes the whole project and we never move on. There is always more to learn, and we need to recognise that we can never learn it all.

The idea for this appendix came to me during a retreat in March 2012, and I spent a month or so praying over the idea, and getting the vision clear in my mind. When I shared the idea with my minister she told me that there was a need, as only during the previous week, two people had shared with her that they were coming up to retirement and wanted to move into full-time Christian or charity work.

The remainder of 2012 was spent in attending seminars and reading books related to the subject, with other information being gleaned from my regular reading. Much of the material in this appendix comes out of my research. Then, of course, there is my own experience of being made redundant, giving me the opportunity of spending eighteen months working with a mission, and facing retirement, giving me the opportunity to do what I am doing now.

As 2012 drew to a close I determined that 2013 would be the year I started to write the appendix, giving myself the deadline of the end of 2014 for completion. I actually started to write the appendix on Boxing Day 2012, and I am in the process of completing it in April 2016. You might think that I took a long time to write an appendix, intended for the closing of a book, but I wanted to take the subject seriously. My long years of working on projects have taught me to be sensible. As a preacher I have sermons to produce, as a leadership trainer I need to give quality time to people, and as world mission coordinator for my church I need to spend time promoting the work of missionaries. If this book is to be my legacy for future generations then I need to take time over it. Work produced under pressure is not the best work.

When we come to retirement, and we want to use our skills and experience in the voluntary sector, we need to make time to look at the possibilities and opportunities available to us. We need to discover the steps we need to take.

If we feel the desire to attend Bible school we need to look at the websites of a number of schools, perhaps sending for the prospectuses of a few, to see what they offer, and if they are suitable for us. If you are in your sixties you might not want to find yourself in a classroom full of teenagers! Some Bible schools run courses especially for older people. When I became redundant from British Coal I attended a course called the Crossroads Discipleship Training School, run by Youth with a Mission. This course was designed for people over thirty-five who had reached a crossroads in their lives. One lady on the course was in her seventies.

If we are feeling the call for overseas missions, we again need to look at the websites of various mission agencies, and send for their magazines and newsletters. If we already have an interest in world missions we may already be receiving magazines, and have a good idea of where we want to go, and what we want to do. Be careful, though. Start your research with an open mind. For around fifteen years or so, I held the very strong feeling that I wanted to be a missionary in Brazil, especially São Paulo. When I joined Youth with a Mission my minister advised me to go in with an open mind. Uganda wasn't even on my radar, but this was the country the mission sent me to. Ever since that time I've been making regular visits to Uganda.

For both Bible school and overseas missions our church leaders need to be fully behind us. They need to see God's calling on our lives, and how suitable a given situation is for us. If we are told that an area is not suitable for us, we are not to take it personally. It is not we who are unsuitable, it's the situation. If God is putting a calling on our lives, and the desire in our hearts, there will be an opening for us. We may need to spend some time finding it, and it may be a million miles from our first thoughts, but there will be an opening for us.

If we have a heart to serve people we may already be involved with a charity in this country in our so-called 'spare time', perhaps in the evenings after completing a day's work. There may be an opportunity, upon retirement, to turn the 'spare time' into full-time. A friend of mine, a serving police officer, was involved with the Boy Scouts in a 'spare time' capacity. Upon retirement from the police force his involvement with the scout movement increased, even to the point of taking groups of boys to international scouting events. He found his fulfilment, after retiring, in something he was already involved with. Don't decry the things you are doing already. Serving God full-time does not necessarily mean a major change in our lives, except perhaps the need for paid work coming to an end.

For all of the above we need to connect with God's vision for our lives. If God isn't with us, then our plans will come to nothing. Proverbs 19, verse 21 says, 'Many plans are in a man's heart, but the LORD's decree will prevail.' Also, in Psalm 127, verse 1, 'Unless the LORD builds a house, its builders labour over it in vain; unless the LORD watches over a city, the watchman stays alert in vain.'

If we are not connected with God's vision for our lives then we will only find frustration. We will find closed door after closed door after closed door. If we do happen to force our way through a closed door we will find the going tough. Our hearts will not be settled. We will feel uncomfortable. We will not feel the peace of fulfilment. We will feel as though we are walking through treacle.

We will have many ideas in our minds. Heeding the

warning in Proverbs 19 quoted above, we need to write these ideas down and bring them before God. The ideas need to be written down in a clear, concise way in order to understand them. I am the world's worst note-taker. I tend to make scribbled notes in my notebook, and when I return to them later, I can't understand them! This is why I'd rather read a book than be lectured at. If something in a book registers with me, I need only to take a note of the page number, and it makes perfect sense when I go back to it.

The best way of getting before God, I find, when needing to take a major decision, especially a potentially life-changing decision, is to take a quiet day. Get off somewhere peaceful, perhaps a favourite spot in the countryside. It is better if nobody knows where we are, and if our mobile phones are turned off. Take only a Bible, a notebook, a pen and the list of options. If there is no café close by we can take a packed lunch and something to drink. Meditate on the list, and on whatever Bible passages come to mind. If any thoughts come into our minds we write them in our notebooks. When we meditate on the thoughts it should become clear if they are from God or not. If one of the options on our list starts to overwhelm the others then we need to investigate it, and perhaps ask trusted friends to pray over it with us. It could be that one of the options was overwhelming our minds anyway, and we simply needed the confirmation. And we should always be open for God dropping an option into our minds that wasn't on the list! God's imagination is far greater than ours!

ARE OUR PLANS PRACTICAL?

Maybe you are coming up to your sixty-fifth birthday and you are looking forward to doing something different. The law in the UK today says that employees are not forced to retire at sixty-five. If we wish, we can carry on. At the time of writing the change in the law has been recent, and many of us have spent twenty years or so looking forward to retirement!

Maybe the industry you are working in is downsizing, perhaps due to a merger or world market prices. It may be cheaper to import the product than it is to produce it in this country! In my mind the latter is a false economy as the situation may change. The world prices may rise, and recent history in the UK has shown that redeployment can be difficult, making an increase of demand upon the benefits system.

For those of us who are Christians there is the matter of 'calling'. That is, God plants in our hearts the desire to enter the ministry, or take our skills overseas on the 'mission field'. This can happen at any age, which opens up a whole new realm of practical issues, particularly regarding finance and support, if we are some way off retirement age.

Or it could be a combination of any of the above. For me it was the combination of God's calling and the industry downsizing. My walk with God started in 1971, and almost immediately, I felt that God might be calling me into full-time Christian work. Due to circumstances the opportunity wasn't arising, and I was feeling frustrated until a wise, elderly Pentecostal pastor suggested to me that God might be leading me through a time of preparation, and that there is quite often a long delay between calling and fulfilment.

During the 1970s and 1980s my employment was as a time and wages clerk with British Coal, and in the 80s, the coal mining industry in the UK was being downsized. Mines were closing, and redundancies were rife. Early in 1989 I asked if there would be the opportunity of being made redundant, and was told that there was no way that clerical staff were being made redundant. As I felt that the time was right to move into the fulfilment of God's calling I prayed over the situation, and in the middle of 1989, the announcement was made that the coal mine I was stationed at was being closed and that there would be vast redundancies. I held my breath.

One morning, those of us working in the offices were called into the manager's office, one by one, to be interviewed by a director. Those of my colleagues who went into the office returned with big smiles on their faces. Then it was my turn to be interviewed, and my turn to smile. The redundancy package I had been offered was too generous to turn down. I left the coal mining industry at the end of 1989, and at the start of 1990, I joined Youth with a Mission.

So, retirement is around the corner, we are in the situation where our pension provides an income, and we want to use our skills and experience in the voluntary sector. Our partner has the same calling and we are both open for God to lead us anywhere in the world.

Of course, the above is only one scenario, and there may be any number of combinations when it comes to retirement. We must remember that everybody's situation is different, and if I try to include each possibility, this appendix would make a book by itself! The reader must adapt!

It could be that our partner has no desire to move overseas, or indeed, they wish to take no part in our venture into the voluntary world. In that case we would be limited to our immediate area. Most areas of the UK, I think, have a wide variety of opportunities to serve. We may find our eyes are opened as we start our research. If we wish to take up church-based work, then the local Churches Together is a good place to start. For opportunities in the secular world, then the local Council for Voluntary Services (CVS) is good. Local government offices, or the local public library, may also have information available.

It could be that we are not of retirement age, but are facing redundancy with a settlement that would make us financially independent for a while. We could be seeing this as an opportunity to take a 'gap year' before seeking further paid work. When I became redundant from British Coal I was able to spend eighteen months with Youth with a Mission before I needed to find paid work. The mission sent me to Kenya and Uganda for five weeks, and I've been making regular visits to Uganda ever since, including a twelve-month 'gap year' when I finally retired from paid work. When I was working I used my annual two weeks' holiday to visit Uganda. A time in voluntary work after redundancy can really change a person's life!

However, back to our original scenario and we are in a position where the future is wide open for us. The first thing we need to do is speak with our church leaders. Ideally, our church leaders will already know that we have a desire to serve God wherever He sends us. My church leaders knew that I had the desire to go overseas for around twenty years before the opportunity arose! Our church leaders will pray for us and with us. They will need to sense our calling for themselves, as they will need to recommend us and give us references. Beware of Bible schools and mission agencies who accept people without references and recommendations from church leaders. You might be in your right mind, but you may find yourself working with an organisation who are off the wall!

Most, if not all, ministers and pastors will have contact with, or know of, mission agencies working overseas and organisations working in this country. We may already have an idea of the missions working in our area of expertise, or the country we are interested in, through mission magazines and newsletters, or through other Christian publications.

Larger churches, and some smaller churches, may have members who have spent time, either overseas or in Britain, with an organisation, and may still have useful contacts. These, and others, should be kept 'in the loop' and may form the basis of a prayer support group. It's important that we have good prayer backing, especially from people who have a heart for the type of life we are seeking to lead. This is especially important if we are destined for overseas service. If possible, try and have somebody in place to deal with practical support, such as maintaining a mailing list for newsletters and dealing with other administrative matters, and who has had experience of the country you are going to, or a similar country. They will understand the issues you are facing.

What type of work do you want to do? Do you want to use the skills you have gained in secular work? Many missionaries I personally know have taken their skills onto the mission field. They are medical people, such as doctors and nurses; teachers, builders and ministers. My secular work was in office management, and I have fulfilled a number of administrative roles in the voluntary sector. Today I preach and offer leadership training, but I'm always open to new opportunities. When I was with Youth with a Mission I served as financial administrator at one of their bases. One weekend, at the financial year end, was spent at the UK head office in Harpenden, helping the accountant with the year-end procedure. The accountant told me that he had been an accountant in secular life, and had joined the mission because he wanted to preach. He wanted to do something different, and became their accountant! If we wish to be obedient to God then we must be willing to fulfil any role He calls us to, even if we wanted to do something different.

What do you do with your house? It was easy for me when I went for my 'gap year'. I was living in rented property and I simply gave my landlord the required notice that I was leaving. But what do we do if we own our house? Maybe we are still paying off a mortgage, which will need keeping up. Do we rent the house out, and risk a tenant who is lax in paying and has no interest in looking after the property? Are we going to find ourselves dealing with serious maintenance matters from thousands of miles away? Do we sell the property? If so, do we wait until it is sold before we go? Or are we happy for an estate agent to deal with it? If we sell our house, where do we live when we return? Do we have the faith that God will us lead to suitable property when we return home? When I returned to Mansfield from my 'gap year' a friend found me a small attic bedsit flat, until, in his words, I 'found something suitable'. I lived in that same flat for six years. God had found my 'something suitable' straight away. Have you the faith for that? God knows exactly what we need.

GETTING PREPARED

We have been given our retirement date, and the countdown is on. Now we need to prepare ourselves for the next big change in our lives. My suggestion, to avoid becoming too anxious, is to treat retirement as a career move or career progression, as it is more positive than 'looking for something to do'. It is good to start preparing ourselves by examining ourselves. We are more complex than any computer and we need to know what makes us tick.

We need to know what our values are. Are we achievement-orientated, with the need to look at a completed project knowing that we are the one responsible for the finished product, or are we people-orientated, happy to encourage others to complete their projects?

What are our interests? Are we artistic, such as in drama or music? There is a piece of film on YouTube which shows me acting with a lady from my church. The lady was good, but I think the director found me a nightmare! Are we academic? Can we prepare sermons and preach? Are we interested in social events? Can we organise fundraising events for charities, such as barn dances or coffee mornings?

What is our personality? According to Myers-Briggs I'm an introvert. I'm also shy with people I don't know. If I'm in a room with people who are strangers to me, somebody has to speak to me first. People who know me well cannot believe that I am shy! It is something I have had to overcome.

What are our skills and strengths? What experience are we bringing from our working lives? Are we willing to learn new skills? Are we able to use our initiative and plan the progress of projects? Do we have interpersonal skills, being able to take up leadership roles? Do we have communication skills, being able to put across what we want in a way that people understand?

What qualifications are we bringing with us, whether they are academic, professional or vocational? When I took a course with Youth with a Mission, one of the leaders was a retired doctor. A friend of mine has a daughter working with a mission in Africa. The daughter, who is well below retirement age, could have been commanding good money as a consultant surgeon had she stayed in the UK, but she has chosen, in obedience to God's calling, to use her skills in a voluntary position in African hospitals.

All the above should be taken into consideration as we look at all the opportunities open to us. As we determine what we offer and what we want, it would be good to discuss with those who know us best, such as family members, colleagues we have worked closely with for a number of years, and close friends.

It is good to create a plan of action, with the help of our church leader or somebody who knows us well. It is useful if the person helping us has had experience in the mission field, or charity work, or the area (whether it is the country or the type of work) we are interested in. The action plan could include an evaluation of what we want, what skills and experience we are offering, and what mission agencies and charities need. We can research the latter through magazines, newsletters and websites. You will probably find yourself with an abundance of opportunities!

Determination will make it happen. Do not be put off by thinking your particular skills cannot be useful. Loren Cunningham had the vision of a ship to carry out mercy-type missions to needy countries, and was praying over the need of skilled staff for the ship. In his book *Is That Really You, Lord?* (Kingsway, 1984) Loren tells of the time he was with a group of people who were praying about the ship. As they were telling God how difficult it would be to find skilled staff, a knock came at the door. When Loren opened the door he found an experienced sea skipper asking how his skills could be used in world missions.

We should ask ourselves what we love to do. There is sometimes a false assumption that God is not interested in the things we love, but will always call us to do something difficult. If we have a desire in our heart, if we have an overwhelming love of a certain area, then it's quite likely that God has put that desire, that love, into our heart. We hear stories where people have refused to get involved with missions in case God sent them to a country they didn't want to go to. If God wants you in a certain country, He will put a love for that country in your heart.

When I visited Africa for the first time in 1990 I hadn't been outside of Britain before in my life. If anybody had asked me if I had been abroad I would have told them that I once went to Anglesey! My flight to Nairobi was my very first time in a plane. We spent our first week in Nairobi, and I didn't like Nairobi one little bit. I wanted to go home!

Then we moved on to Eldoret, and this was better. My feeling whilst in Eldoret was that if God was calling me to Eldoret, then I wouldn't mind.

Then we crossed over the border from Kenya into Uganda, and I knew I was where God wanted me to be. We spent two and a half weeks on a Youth with a Mission base on the edge of Jinja, and as we crossed the border back into Kenya, I knew I would be returning to Uganda.

We need to ask ourselves what gives us a real sense of purpose, what gives us satisfaction? What are we doing when we feel fulfilled? At the time of writing I am feeling more fulfilled than I ever have before in my life. Paid, secular work is behind me, and my time is spent with preaching, offering leadership training and promoting world mission. I am satisfied that I am fulfilling God's purpose for my life. This book will probably be my legacy for future generations. That is the hope that drives me on as I put finger to keyboard.

We need to consider the gifts that we have. My first thought when I consider my gifts is that I haven't got any. Then I remember the experiences God has brought me through in my working life, and in my church life. The gifts we have are by God's grace. If God wants us to do something then He will give us the ability to do it.

We need to be realistic, though, as we consider our gifts. What we can and cannot do should be obvious. For example, it would be no good for me to take on a maintenance role. My DIY skills make Frank Spencer look like an expert! My friend Geoff has banned me from owning a tool kit, as he's tired of sorting out all the messes I make! We consider our gifts, and offer them to God to be used. God equips us for what He wants us to do. He does not equip us for those tasks we take on that are outside of His calling.

Then we look at the things we love to do, at the times we feel a real sense of purpose and satisfaction, and at the gifts we have and see how it all fits in with God's picture. We develop our purpose statement based upon these things and use it as our frame, or blueprint.

GET ON WITH IT

In the November 2012 edition of Reader's Digest, Phil Redmond, chair of National Museums Liverpool, wrote that he could see the benefits that were gained by volunteers contributing to the workforce. He said that a job is much more than a paycheque.

Even in a voluntary position we generally have to attend interviews before being accepted. After all, the organisation needs to know that we are going to be an asset, not a burden. Charities and missions exist to serve other people, not members of their own staff. The best way is to treat it as a job interview.

The saying 'first impressions count' applies when it comes to interviews for a position. It is said that when we meet somebody for the first time we make eleven conclusions in the first seven seconds. A good television commercial can sell a product in thirty seconds, and that is how long we have to sell ourselves.

Put yourself in the shoes of the person who is interviewing you. Having sat on both sides of the desk (I've interviewed people for jobs as well as applied for jobs myself), I can tell you that the interviewer is every bit as nervous as the interviewee. After all, they don't want to make a mistake by offering the job to somebody who is unsuitable and who will cost the organisation a lot of money and trouble. Personally, I'm the world's worst interviewer as I'm liable to give the job to the first person who comes through the door!

The interviewer generally has four question areas, which apply equally to paid work and volunteer positions. They want to know if we are able to do the job. That follows on to the question of whether we will do the job. There is a difference between being able to do a job and being willing to do a job. Even voluntary organisations can't afford people who are only along for the ride. They will need to see that we will fit into the organisation. Can we get along with people? Do we share the organisation's ethos? It's no good joining an animal rescue centre if we dislike animals. And what potential can the interviewer see in us? Any good manager, whether it's a business or a charity, wants to see his staff develop. Even if we have 'retired' from paid work, there is still room for growth. There is always room for growth.

There are also four question areas about which the applicant can ask the interviewer. We can ask about the role. Of course we know what position we have applied for, but we can ask about the specifics. We can ask about the organisation and their areas of work. We base these questions on what we have already gleaned from internet sites and publications issued by the organisation. It would be bad to go into the interview knowing nothing at all about the mission or charity. We can ask about the next steps. How long can we expect to wait before receiving a reply? Will there be further interviews, or an assessment weekend? During a seminar I attended on career advancement we were told that a good question would be to ask the interviewer what made them join the company! I wish I'd known about that one when I was job-hunting!

As we prepare for retirement it's good to sit back

and reflect upon our dreams and thoughts of the future. There are questions we need to ask ourselves, such as: what do we need to do to prepare for the next step? What opportunities are there before us that we can investigate? What options are there that we have not yet considered?

We also need to identify somebody who will come alongside us to encourage us, and truthfully evaluate our strengths and achievements. The evaluation needs to be truthful to prevent us from becoming too ambitious, or underselling ourselves.

One of my sayings is, 'I have a problem with procrastination, but we can deal with it some other time.' If God has called you, and you know God has called you, and you know what He wants you to do and where He wants you to do it, then GET ON WITH IT! And may God bless you abundantly.

ACKNOWLEDGMENTS

A book doesn't write itself, and a writer can't work alone. The writer is taking ideas on board from a wide range of resources. Style is taken from other books, and ideas are taken from conversations.

However, some people make a special effort to help and their help is invaluable. I started to write the book in 1992 and received tremendous help and advice from Rev. Roger Borlace, Alastair Murray (now deceased) and Anne Barke. Additions were made in 2001 during the time between suffering a heart attack and waiting for heart surgery. Geoff Carlin, Ian Bown and Karen Sheeran (now Thorpe) read through and made welcome suggestions as to readability and grammar. Thank you to the people mentioned above. A special thank you is expressed to all at Matador for their expert help in publishing this book.

Thanks are expressed to you, if you have bought a copy of this book. I hope you enjoy reading it as much as I enjoyed living it.

Most of all, I give thanks to our Lord Jesus Christ for His hand on my life.

I just want to give a note about presentation. I am aware that I have jumped between past tense and present tense. When I have written in past tense I am describing events as they were at the time they happened, and the situation is different now, as far as I am aware. When I have written in present tense, the situation, again, as far as I am aware, is still the same at the time of writing the final draft.